1972

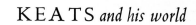

KEATS *and his world*

KEATS *and his world*

BY TIMOTHY HILTON

A STUDIO BOOK

THE VIKING PRESS · NEW YORK

To Nuala O'Faolain

Copyright © *1971 Thames and Hudson Ltd London*

Published in 1971 by The Viking Press, Inc.
625 Madison Avenue, New York, N.Y. 10022

SBN 670–41196–5

Library of Congress catalog card number: 78–146972

Printed and bound in Great Britain by Jarrold and Sons Ltd, Norwich, England

George (*left*) and Tom Keats, sketched by John's friend Severn in 1817. 'They seemed to think their Brother John was to be exalted, & to exalt the family name.'

(*Right*) Fanny Keats as she appeared in later life, when married to the Spaniard Valentin Maria Llanos y Gutierrez; the portrait is by her son. In his very last letter Keats wrote of her, 'my sister – who walks about my imagination like a ghost – she is so like Tom.'

JOHN KEATS was born in 1795, in the parish of Moorfields, within sight of St Paul's, almost within sound of Bow Bells. His father, Thomas Keats, had married Frances Jennings in the previous year. There were five children of the marriage. George was born in 1797, Tom in 1799, and Frances, known always as Fanny, in 1803. Edward died in his infancy. Thomas Keats, who came of West of England stock, had a position of some responsibility, managing his father-in-law's thriving livery stables at the Swan and Hoop in Moorfields. John Keats' earliest years would have been spent among the warming bustle of hospitality, of comings and goings, of steaming horses in the cobbled yard.

Family

Thomas Keats is sometimes described as an ostler, but this does not give a true picture of his social standing. If the Keats family were in no sense well connected, they were certainly of a prosperous class, and were not short of money. Thomas Keats would often have worked with his sleeves rolled up, but he ran a successful business, one from which his father-in-law had retired with a modest fortune. Thomas saw to it that his own children were well educated. He considered sending John to Harrow, where there were many of the sons of successful London

5

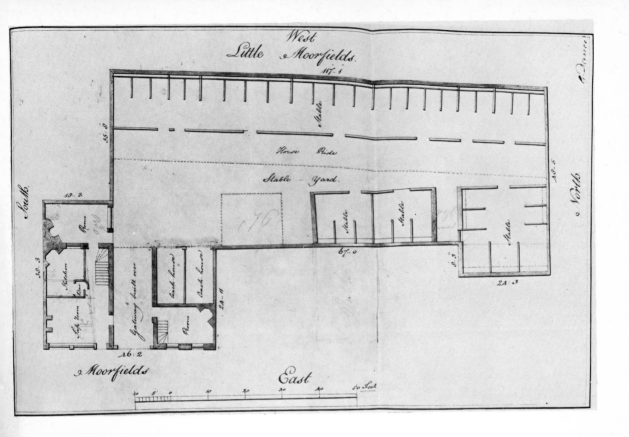

Within the plan (as labelled):

West

Little Moorfields.

South. ... *North.*

Stable

Horse Ride

Stable - Yard.

Stable

Stable

Stable

Stable

Kitchen

Room

Gateway built over

Coach house

Coach house

Room

Moorfields

East

Plan of the Swan and Hoop: the stable-yard was approached by a covered passage next to the public-house – an arrangement visible in Chew's livery stables and the King's Arms (*left*) on the other side of Little Moorfields. The paler marks show alterations proposed by Keats' mother when she took over at the death of her father in 1804

tradesmen. But in the event John was placed, with George, in a small private school in Enfield, some seven miles north of the City.

It seems to have been an excellent school, and one with a remarkably liberal atmosphere. Its headmaster, John Clarke, looked over his seventy or eighty boys with a kindly eye. There was no beating, and there were many other books besides schoolbooks. John Clarke's young son, Charles, who helped with the teaching, was to direct Keats' reading towards the treasures of English at a crucial stage in the poet's early development. Charles recalled the school as having 'a garden, one hundred yards in length, where in one corner were some plots set apart for certain boys fond of having a garden of their own.' There was a pond, a rustic arbour, and 'beyond this, a gate led into a small field, or paddock, of two acres – the pasture ground of two cows that supplied the establishment with fresh and abundant milk.' The Keats' parents, in a gig, often drove out to visit their sons.

But while John was still eight years old his father, returning alone from such a visit, was unseated from his horse, fractured his skull, and died. His wife remarried within three months, but seems not to have made a fortunate choice. She soon left her new husband; the four children went to live with her mother, who, recently widowed herself, had moved to Edmonton, a small Middlesex village very near to Enfield.

Clarke's school

Clarke's school at Enfield. In Keats' time the house, built in 1717, was surrounded by a garden

According to one of his contemporaries, John Keats gave the impression at school that he was marked out for a military career. He seems to have been a boisterous lad, always fighting. But there were also signs of an ardent and emotional spirit. His schoolfellow also recalled 'the generosity and daring of his character . . . in passions of tears or outrageous fits of laughter always in extremes will help to paint Keats in his boyhood.' When his mother died in March 1810 he huddled silently under John Clarke's desk, inconsolable; his feeling of loss was 'impassioned and prolonged'.

The inheritance   The four Keats children were orphaned when John, the eldest, was fourteen years old. Their grandmother sensibly decided to settle money on them, and to appoint a guardian and trustee. Her choice was Richard Abbey, a City tea merchant whom she had known for some years, and to him she made over some £9000, a large part of the money that she had inherited from her husband. Initially there was one more trustee, but he took little part in these matters, and it was to be Abbey that controlled the young family's fortunes, both financially and in the choice of their careers. His unfeeling attitude towards the Keats children, no less than his tight-fisted handling of their money, proved to be a continual difficulty in their lives.

It was probably Abbey who curtailed their education. John and George were removed from school in 1810. George was put to work in Abbey's counting-house in Pancras Lane. John, however, was apprenticed to his grandparents' doctor,

Inspection of the Honourable Artillery Company in 1803, on their Finsbury parade ground near the Swan and Hoop

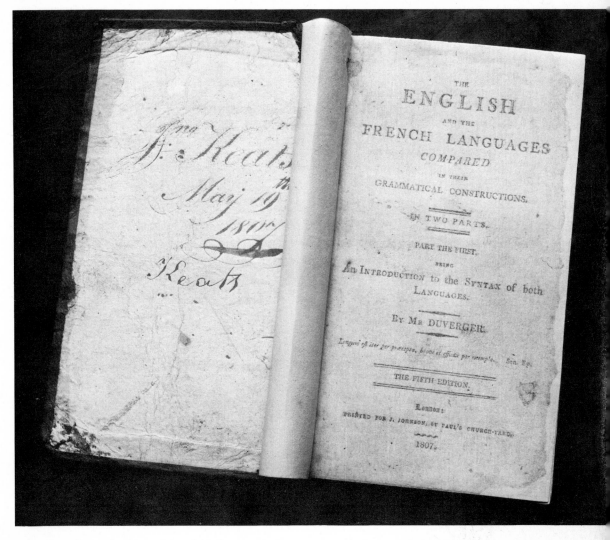

One of Keats' schoolbooks, with his childish signature. It was comparatively rare to find modern languages taught in schools of the day

the surgeon and apothecary Thomas Hammond. The future poet was to spend the next five years of his life serving an apprenticeship in a trade—a trade more than a profession—totally unconnected with literature. In contrast with his unsettled childhood and the vigorously active months of his young maturity, these years were, as Charles Cowden Clarke pointed out, 'the most placid period of his painful life.'

9

Apprenticeship   We know little about the circumstances of his life as an apprentice. He moved to live above Hammond's surgery in Edmonton, only a few yards from his grand-mother's house. He probably performed the usual duties of a surgeon's apprentice, looking after a multiplicity of odd jobs, being allowed to help his master as he went about the more specialized aspects of his business, and learning elementary medical matters. All this had little effect on his imagination. Far more important was the way he continued his schooldays, reading under the personal supervision of Charles Cowden Clarke. Once or twice a week, Keats would leave the surgery in the late afternoon and walk the two miles through the lanes and field-paths to Enfield, where he would meet Clarke to return and borrow books, mainly the works of the English poets. They would talk about them for hours. Late in the evening, Clarke often walked half-way home with his young friend.

Clarke's influence was not solely literary, though one can hardly underestimate the importance of his giving Keats that sort of rapturous taste for books, 'high-piled . . . like full garners', that was always to characterize the poet. He also gave Keats his politics. We can point to a specific source for the liberal and progressive views that Keats held in Leigh Hunt's journal *The Examiner*, to which Clarke

Thomas Hammond's house (*below right*) and surgery in Edmonton. The surgery lay to the right of the house, reached by a cobbled path: the open door is that of the dispensary, with the apprentices' quarters above it

A country path and stile near Enfield ▶

near Enfield.

Day & Haghe, Lith^{rs} to the Queen.

London Published by Rowney, Dillon & Rowney, 51 Rathbone Place.

Charles Cowden Clarke in about 1834, with busts of Shakespeare and Chaucer behind him. After his years as a schoolmaster Clarke became a publisher and a lecturer on literary topics. The best-known concordance to Shakespeare was published by his wife in 1845

was devoted and which he circulated—to Abbey's horror—among the older boys in the school. In the context of the times, when England was nearer to violent uprising than in any other period of her history, one can hardly call this *mélange* of political and literary opinion a 'radical' paper. It had none of the revolutionary fervour, and little of the working-class audience, of such publications as Thomas Wooler's *Black Dwarf*, beside which it appears as the product of a political dilet-tante. But it was lively and courageous, and a constant critic of the Tory govern-ment of Liverpool, Sidmouth and Castlereagh. The paper was edited by two brothers, John and Leigh Hunt, who continually ran the risk of action against them for their unsparing derogation of those in high places. In 1811 they were brought to trial for their attack on military flogging, but were acquitted. In 1814 they were finally imprisoned for a libellous assault on the despised Prince Regent.

Like Clarke, Keats became a zealous reader of *The Examiner*. It bolstered both a natural pugnacity and a genuine feeling for the troubles of the lower classes and, for a time, instilled in him a general taste for social disaffection. A somewhat disapproving contemporary later noted of him, using typically Tory phraseology, that he 'was not one of those who thought it better to bear the ills we have, than

Keats' copy of Spenser's *Faerie Queene*.
Brown wrote, 'In Spenser's fairy land
he was enchanted, breathed in a new
world, and became another being.'

fly to others which we know not of. He was of the sceptical and republican school.
An advocate for the innovations that were making progress in his time. A fault-
finder with everything established.'

When Keats was eighteen years old he wrote his first poetry, a few stanzas in
imitation of Spenser. It is a bower-of-bliss type of poetry, full of obviously poetical
effects and reminiscences:

First poetry

> *Now Morning from her orient chamber came,*
> *And her first footsteps touch'd a verdant hill;*
> *Crowning its lawny crest with amber flame,*
> *Silv'ring the untainted gushes of its rill . . .*

We know that Spenser was one of the poets that Keats had read most enthusiastically when discussing literature with Charles Cowden Clarke. Keats read the
Epithalamion and then *The Faerie Queene*, which he approached 'as a young horse
would through a spring meadow,-ramping!' Clarke also records how Keats
responded-physically-to the magic quality of Spenser's epithets: 'He hoisted himself up, and looked burly and dominant, as he said, "What an image that is,-

13

'*Sea-shouldering whales*'!"' Keats' physical movement at the excitement of the poetry suggests the young Coleridge who walked through the streets of London, oblivious to passers-by, making swimming motions with his arms: he was imagining himself in the Hellespont, having just read Marlowe's *Hero and Leander*. Many stories remind us that Keats' feeling for poetry could often occupy him in just this sort of way; a kind of swooning leap into the poetic, which is a Romantic characteristic.

Spenser, Keats' first love, has always been known as a 'poet's poet', and there are many Romantic tributes to him; one thinks of Wordsworth's recollections of reading him at Cambridge –

> *Sweet Spenser, moving through his clouded heaven*
> *With the moon's beauty and the moon's soft pace*

– of Coleridge's discussion of his allegory and 'indescribable sweetness and fluent projection'; and one thinks of course of the many Romantic poems that were directly influenced by him. Keats' poems were among these; and an important part of his early reading was not only in Spenser himself but also in his imitators, in poems like James Beattie's *The Minstrel*, which combines an eighteenth-century progress-of-poetry theme with a Romantic medievalism, and Mrs Tighe's *Psyche* of 1805, which actually gave many hints to Keats. But in Mrs Tighe especially we are aware that it is possible to drown in Spenserianism, and Keats was indeed in danger of this for some time. Spenser and the Spenserians are responsible for most of the affected and over-lush parts of his early writing. Keats' own poetic good sense – for he was a fine critic of poetry – no less than his developing creative powers, later convinced him that, as Hazlitt expressed it, Spenser's poetry 'is inspired by the love of ease, and relaxation from all the cares and businesses of life', and that he 'could lull the senses into a deep oblivion of the jarring noises of the world.' An important part of Keats' poetic development was always to be in the substitution of more demanding poetic models – as in his later use of that very different 'poet's poet', Dryden.

Keats also experimented with sonnets at this time, and they too are essentially derivative poems. He wrote one, *On Peace*, in which his response to the end of the Napoleonic Wars is conveyed in rather mechanical eighteenth-century abstractions. Others were addressed to Byron and Chatterton. Another, much influenced by Milton, was that *Written on the Day that Mr. Leigh Hunt Left Prison*, and this poem he shyly gave to Cowden Clarke. At about this time he seems to have quarrelled with Hammond, and moved away from the surgery to rooms of his own. Practically all of Keats' life was to be spent in lodgings.

Guy's Hospital   In the autumn of 1815, his apprenticeship at an end, Keats' medical career took another step forward when he registered at Guy's Hospital and commenced a training in surgical practice. He joined whole-heartedly in the rounds of hospital

The vast complex of Guy's (*right*) and St Thomas' hospitals appears to the left in the map below. Keats first lived between the hospitals at No. 28 St Thomas' Street (left of the brewery entrance); later he moved to No. 8 Dean Street, next to a Nonconformist chapel, shaded at the far right of the plan

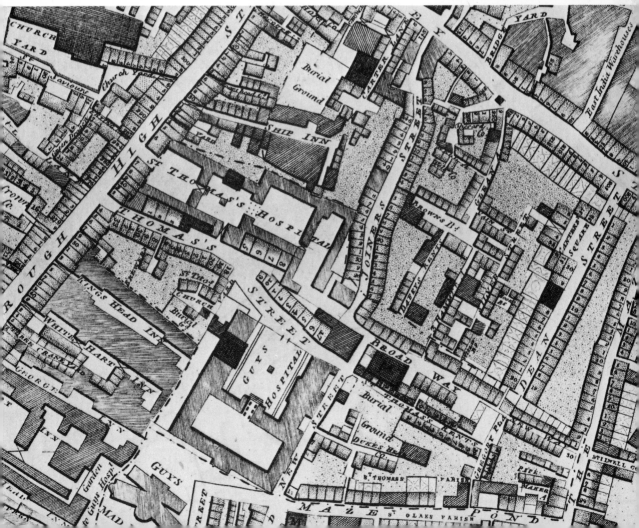

tance to see the remains, till the body was so changed that
she with difficulty recognised it to be her brother's, and
the blood was then oozing through the shroud.

TO SOLITUDE.

O SOLITUDE! if I must with thee dwell,
    Let it not be among the jumbled heap
    Of murky buildings;—climb with me the steep,
Nature's Observatory—whence the dell,
Its flowery slopes—its rivers crystal swell,
    May seem a span : let me thy vigils keep
    'Mongst boughs pavilioned ; where the Deer's swift leap
Startles the wild Bee from the Fox-glove bell.
Ah ! fain would I frequent such scenes with thee ;
    But the sweet converse of an innocent mind,
    Whose words are images of thoughts refin'd,
Is my soul's pleasure ; and it sure must be
    Almost the highest bliss of human kind,
When to thy haunts two kindred spirits flee.

                    J. K

Keats' first published poem, in *The Examiner* for May 1816

with attention. He learnt from Leigh Hunt's recently published *Story of Rimini*, and incorporated some of its artifices in his own fragmentary romance *Calidore*. He also embarked on those lines which open so nimbly with 'I stood tip-toe upon a little hill', his first attempt at a kind of poetic self-exploration that was to become increasingly important to him. But Keats had muddled intentions about this poem. He took it up and he put it aside, and for a time even referred to it as 'Endymion', thinking that he might develop some narrative around the story of the shepherd boy of Mount Latmos. The poem originated in a simple feeling of delight in a particular place. Hunt says it was suggested 'by a delightful summer day, as he stood beside the gate that leads from the Battery on Hampstead Heath into a field by Caen Wood' (the old spelling of Kenwood). The opening lines, the three long sentences that form the first paragraph of verse, are delightful: Keats seems to be writing above himself, with a freshness of observation that is far removed from the repetitions and usages of poeticizing stock. But this is not sustained; and, apart from some important hints of a human Grecian splendour in the last lines (which were actually written a few months later), the rest of the poem is undistinguished—on occasion embarrassingly so.

Medicine versus poetry   Keats' natural quickness of mind enabled him to follow the medical courses with ease. But there was less and less chance of an emotional commitment to medicine. The attractions of poetry were becoming stronger. Keats dramatized this conflict, in somewhat affected manner, when he remarked to Cowden Clarke that 'the other day, for instance, during the lecture, there came a sunbeam in the room, and with it a whole troop of creatures floating in the ray; and I was off with them to Oberon and Fairy-land.' There seems little doubt that Keats' poetical

18

Keats in 1816, by Severn. For him at this time, Stephens wrote, 'The greatest men in the world were the Poets, and to rank among them was the chief object of his ambition. – It may readily be imagined that this feeling was accompanied with a good deal of Pride and some conceit, and that amongst mere Medical students, he would walk, & talk as one of the Gods might be supposed to do, when mingling with mortals.'

Lecture notes (on the anatomy of the head) and floral distractions in Keats' medical notebook

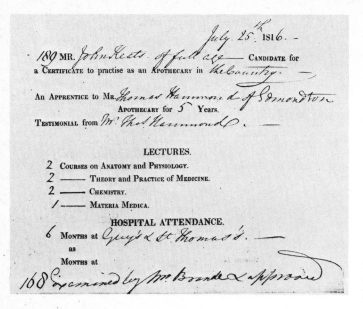

Certificate of the Society of Apothecaries, allowing Keats to practise medicine outside London

fancies were constricted by the noise and squalor around him, in this most turbulent quarter of London. He determined to get away, and did so as soon as he had sat his apothecary examinations in July 1816.

Keats had never seen the sea. The manner in which he chose to do so may seem typically Cockney, for he puffed down the Thames estuary and along the Kent coast in a steamer bound for Margate, at that date just becoming a popular resort for Londoners. Tom went with him. When they disembarked they found promenades, a theatre, crowded beaches and bathing-machines. But Margate was still a small town; as the brothers stood on the front they could see cornfields that came right down to the edges of the cliffs. Two months later, when they left for home, it was almost harvest-time. At Margate Keats wrote some sonnets and the verse epistles *To my Brother George*, *To Charles Cowden Clarke*, and *To George Felton Mathew*.

Verse letters   The form of the poetic letter had probably been suggested by Leigh Hunt; many of his rhyming epistles had recently appeared in *The Examiner*. And it was a form that perfectly suited the occasion, for Keats was separated, at a postman's distance, from those two or three friends with a sympathetic interest in his youthful attempts at versifying. Letters between friends are the least formal of literary occasions. There are no rules for them, and no conventions. Keats' long Margate poems follow no set pattern, and are essentially friendly poems not only in their tone, but also in their expectation of the reader's sympathy, for they are unabashedly concerned with personal ambition, however much their surface is occupied by

20

The sea front at Margate; holidaymakers bathed in private from the bathing machines, drawn into the water by horses. Keats was depressed by the town's lack of trees

conventional poetic properties. The *Epistle to my Brother George* opens with worries, with a dramatization of his need to write and his inability to do so. It continues with a discussion of the poet's visionary abilities (which are very nearly equated with simple personal pleasures – a thing that often happens in early Keats) and a rather over-grand vision of the poet's effect on posterity:

> *The patriot shall feel*
> *My stern alarum, and unsheath his steel;*
> *Or, in the Senate thunder out my numbers*
> *To startle princes from their easy slumbers*

– a thought that may seem to derive from the inflated rhetoric of *The Examiner*. The verse letter *To Charles Cowden Clarke* has a similar theme, but is a much surer piece. While a blatantly self-conscious poem, it has an extremely touching description of the value of Clarke's encouragement, with something of that manly tenderness that is so marked a feature of Keats' capacity for personal friendship, and it is quite without the striving and sense of strain that make one feel that the letter to George would need to be read out in rather a loud voice. It is a poem that meanders somewhat, but it hardly suffers from its digressions, and successfully communicates, in this relaxed, protracted, almost conversational way of writing, Keats' hankering after a poetic subject. For at this stage, like many another young writer, he was filled with those feelings known as 'poetic' feelings, but lacked a specific subject or occasion that could marshal them into a single, self-contained poem.

Such an occasion was soon to present itself. The Keats brothers went back to London at the beginning of October 1816. John found new rooms at No. 8 Dean Street, Southwark, next to St Thomas' Hospital, a 'beastly place' as he described it, full of 'dirt, turnings and windings'. He was anxious to look up Clarke, now living in Camberwell, and a few days later spent a memorable time with him. Clarke had borrowed the 1610 folio edition of Chapman's translation of Homer. They stayed up all night, thrilled with it, reading to each other. Keats walked home at dawn, did not go to bed, but sat down to write. Tired, he marked out on the side of his page the rhyme-scheme divisions of a Petrarchan sonnet. With this *'Chapman's* rough guide he then wrote *On first looking into Chapman's Homer*, with only one *Homer'* correction. He found an early postal messenger, and the poem was on Clarke's breakfast-table when he came downstairs at ten o'clock that morning. It is the first of Keats' major poems, fluent, muscular, confidently assimilating the influence of his reading.

(*Left*) One of the seventeenth-century slums in Southwark, Boar's Head Place, to the north of St Thomas' Hospital

(*Right*) Keats' draft of *On first looking into Chapman's Homer*, written on a scrap of paper, with the rhyme-scheme marked on the right. Only one line, the seventh, was altered before its publication in 1817

On the first looking into Chapman's Homer

Much have I travell'd in the Realms of Gold,
And many goodly States, and Kingdoms seen;
Round many Western islands have I been,
Which Bards in featly to Apollo hold.
Of one wide expanse had I been told,
Which deep brow'd Homer ruled as his Demesne:
Yet could I never judge what Men could mean,
Till I heard Chapman speak out loud and bold.
Then felt I like some Watcher of the Skies
When a new Planet swims into his Ken,
Or like stout Cortez, when with wond'ring eyes
He star'd at the Pacific, and all his Men
Look'd at each other with a wild surmise —
Silent upon a Peak in Darien —

Leigh Hunt, drawn by
Wageman just after his release
from prison in February 1815.
Wageman was known for his
portraits of actors

Leigh Hunt   A few days later Clarke took him to meet Leigh Hunt. They walked from Dean Street to Hampstead, Keats all eagerness. Hunt and Keats took to each other immediately. 'We became intimate on the spot,' said Hunt, 'and I found the young poet's heart as warm as his imagination.' Keats called three more times in the next few days; and then a bed was made up for him on a sofa in Hunt's library. He became a member of the household.

Hunt, with his particular brand of easy sentiment, has often seemed a lightweight. His prose writings have a diffuse self-indulgence; he wrote soft poetry. Sometimes he appears absurd. He carried a little book of verse to his trial, and painted his prison rooms to represent a green bower. *The Story of Rimini* sometimes plunges into such renowned bathos as

> *The two divinest things this world has got*
> *A lovely woman in a rural spot.*

A little of this type of lax poeticizing undoubtedly rubbed off on the youthful Keats. It is one reason why he is occasionally regarded as a flower-picking, rambling sort of poet, a Cockney tripper in a self-made sylvan elysium. Keats himself later came to despise this early influence on his imagination, and indeed said some surprisingly harsh things about Hunt. But this is to take the hard view. We should remember that Hunt was perceptive and generous, always interested in young

24

poets, and always willing to help them. Keats' friendship with Hunt almost certainly took him out of medicine, as contact with a more experienced man of letters solidified his growing sense of the poetic vocation.

Keats is always associated with Hampstead. He came to feel that the village was his home largely because of the warm welcome that Hunt gave him. The editor of *The Examiner* had always loved Hampstead, which he often apostrophized in verse:

> *A steeple issuing from a leafy rise,*
> *With farmy fields in front, and sloping green,*
> *Dear Hampstead . . .*

Hunt's cottage was in the Vale of Health, a charming little valley in the Heath, a 'nestling spot' indeed. Here was the companionship and conversation of a man who, Keats must surely have thought, was in every respect the opposite of his mean-minded guardian Richard Abbey. Here too were pictures and prints, and we now

Hampstead in 1828/30: Wentworth Place is by the ponds on the right (Keats Grove was then Albion Grove), with Pond Street to the south. To the north are the Vale of Health, and Millfield Walk (between the E and A of 'Hampstead') leading towards Kenwood. Bottom left is West End, where Fanny Brawne was born

The Vale of Health. Hunt's is the large double house on the left

The visual arts find the first indication of the immense stimulus that Keats was to derive from the visual arts, for the final lines of *Sleep and Poetry*, written in the Vale of Health, describe the pictures hanging in the library where he often stayed the night—reproductions of Claude, Poussin and Titian.

Keats was moving away from the life of a medical practitioner towards a life dominated by art, and two more new acquaintances were to assist in the transformation. The first was Benjamin Robert Haydon, a painter with a truly huge conception of the artistic calling. The other was a young literary man of much his own age, John Hamilton Reynolds, who was to become Keats' closest friend.

26

Titian's *Bacchus and Ariadne*, of which
Keats saw a print at Hunt's. In *Sleep and
Poetry* he writes of

> *the swift bound*
> *Of Bacchus from his chariot, when his eye*
> *Made Ariadne's cheek look blushingly*

The *Triumph of Flora*, engraved after
Poussin. In a sonnet to Leigh Hunt,
Keats laments that they will see

> *No crowd of nymphs soft voic'd and*
> *young and gay,*
> *In woven baskets bringing ears of corn,*
> *Roses, and pinks, and violets, to adorn*
> *The shrine of Flora in her early May.*

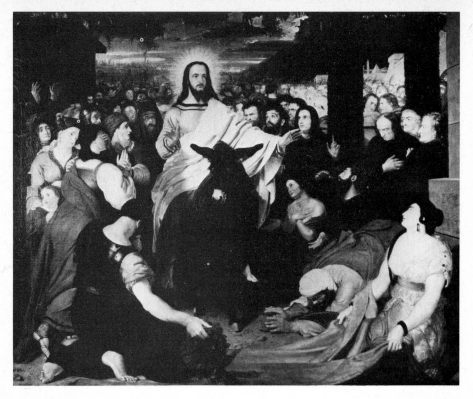

Christ's Entry into Jerusalem. In Haydon's huge painting can be seen, on the right, portraits of Keats (in profile, between the dark pillars), Wordsworth, Voltaire and Newton; Hazlitt appears, with stubbled chin, above Christ's left hand

Benjamin Robert Haydon

Keats met Haydon at Hunt's, and the experience must have been overwhelming. Haydon felt himself to be almost on speaking terms with the gods. He was totally convinced of his own genius. 'What fire, what magic!', he remarked of his own painting. He felt himself called to be the English successor to Raphael and Michel-angelo, men of his own stature. He wrote in his journal that 'never have I had such irresistible, perpetual and continued urgings of future greatness. I have been like a man with air balloons under his armpits and ether in his soul.' Haydon's grandiose conception of his own powers was shared, almost, by his contemporaries. 'High is our calling, Friend!', said Wordsworth. Hunt wrote a sonnet in Haydon's copy of Vasari's *Lives of the Painters*, comparing him with the masters of the High Renaissance. Keats himself joined the chorus of praise in his sonnet 'Great spirits now on earth are sojourning', written after a visit to the painter's studio in Great Marlborough Street, where Haydon was working on his enormous canvas of *Christ's Entry into Jerusalem*. Haydon was soon to incorporate a vivid portrait of Keats into this picture, for he had a scarcely less exalted view of the poet's powers. Significantly, perhaps, Haydon's view of Keats was based more on his impression

28

Benjamin Robert Haydon in 1816, a
self-portrait

A page from Haydon's diary, which
includes sketches for *Christ's Entry into
Jerusalem* and, in the top centre profile, a
'vile caricature' of Haydon by Keats

John Hamilton Reynolds. 'Upon my soul', Keats
wrote to him, 'I have been getting more and more
close to you every day, ever since I knew you.'
Reynolds introduced Keats to Brown, Rice, Bailey,
Taylor and Hessey. On his tombstone is simply
inscribed 'The friend of Keats'

of the poet's personality than on a knowledge of his writing, for Keats had written
little that he would wish to show to such a man. At all events, Haydon wrote
that 'Keats is the only man I ever met with who is conscious of a high call . . .
except Wordsworth, but Keats is more my own age. . . . We saw through each
other *at once*, and I hope in God are friends for ever.'

Keats was inspired by Haydon's largeness of spirit. His other new friend, John
Hamilton Reynolds, enlivened him, introduced him to people, and taught him
a kind of sophistication and independence of judgement. Reynolds was employed
as a junior clerk in an insurance office, and was soon to enter the law – a 'dreary
profession', as he called it. But he was also a literary man: when Keats made
his acquaintance he had already published books of verse and had written a
successful farce. One of his talents, characteristically, was for parody, and his gibing
take-offs of the Wordsworth of *Lyrical Ballads* are very funny. His wit and sharp
apprehensions made him particularly entertaining company. But his was not a
superficial mind; some of Keats' most deeply thought letters are addressed to him.

Keats disliked living in Dean Street. After spending little more than a month
there, he moved with his two brothers – Fanny was still at boarding-school – to
76 Cheapside, in the heart of the City of London. Tom's health was beginning
to give worry, so much so that he had given up working in Abbey's counting-
house; George was still there, however, chafing at the routine and lack of
opportunity. This November Keats wrote a sonnet, *To my Brothers*, that is full
of images of home and fireside, and touchingly describes their domestic circum-

John Hamilton
Reynolds

30

stances and the warm affection they felt for each other. This kind of brotherly affection was indeed exceptional, as Keats realized when he wrote that 'my love for my brothers from the early loss of our parents and even for earlier misfortunes has grown into an affection "passing the love of women".'

On 31 October 1816 Keats had celebrated his twenty-first birthday. His majority renewed the question of his future career. He had little wish either to practise as an apothecary or to set up as a surgeon, possibilities equally open to him. He went to discuss matters with Abbey, his mind firmly fixed on poetry.

We know of the famous interview with Abbey only through a second-hand report, but it is a reliable account of their conversation. Abbey was naturally anxious that Keats should make use of his training, and Keats was equally determined not to do so:

Not intend to be a surgeon! why what do you mean to be? I mean to rely upon my abilities as a poet—John you are either mad or a fool to talk in so absurd a manner. My mind is made up, said the youngster very quietly. I know

Cheapside, looking west towards St Mary Le Bow. No. 76 is on the left side of the street; John and Tom's sitting-room windows, on the first floor, are just to the right of the streetlamp

that I possess abilities greater than most men, and therefore I am determined to gain my living by exercising them – Seeing nothing could be done Abbey called him a silly boy and prophesied a speedy termination to his inconsiderate enterprise.

Especially noteworthy in this account is Keats' confidence. This belief in his own powers was largely the product of an instinctive self-knowledge that we often notice in him. It was bolstered by the support of his friends, and particularly by an article of Hunt's which appeared in December 1816. This article was entitled 'Young Poets', and discussed the work of Keats for the first time, together with that of Reynolds and Shelley. This was a proud moment for Keats. Furthermore, plans were now going ahead for the publication, by the brothers Charles and James Ollier, of Keats' first book of verse, and he was working hard – mainly at Hunt's – to complete *Sleep and Poetry*, a poem which has some of the characteristics of an artistic credo.

'Sleep and Poetry' *Sleep and Poetry* continues and enlarges some of the concerns which had first been expressed in the Margate verse letters, and contains a discussion of nature, of the poetic tradition, and of the present state of poetry. But to say that it discusses these topics is perhaps to suggest an intellectual control that was not really present. For *Sleep and Poetry* has little organized thought in it, and many of its best moments are at precisely those points where argument is abandoned – like the fertile succession of images following the cry 'Stop and consider!', with their rapid and discrete catalogue of 'a poor Indian's sleep', 'A pigeon tumbling in clear summer air', 'A laughing school-boy . . . Riding the springy branches of an elm.' *Sleep and Poetry* is about writing, but Keats now shows how much he is conscious of the insufficiency of those posies of poesy that he could bind together with such disarming facility:

> *Yes, I must pass them for a nobler life,*
> *Where I may find the agonies, the strife*
> *Of human hearts . . .*

However, this is followed by some fifty lines of attack on eighteenth-century poetry, lines whose superficiality and adolescent intolerance were to make Byron, among others, scornful of Keats' half-educated culture. Borrowing a phrase from Hazlitt, Keats condemned the poets who used the classic heroic couplet (Byron, it may be recalled, idolized Pope):

> *They sway'd about upon a rocking horse,*
> *And thought it Pegasus.*

He follows this with a spirited but somewhat silly attack on 'one Boileau', of whom he knew next to nothing. Hunt may well have mentioned him to Keats,

32

'My awful Visage': the life-mask of Keats made by ▶
Haydon in December 1816 (actual size)

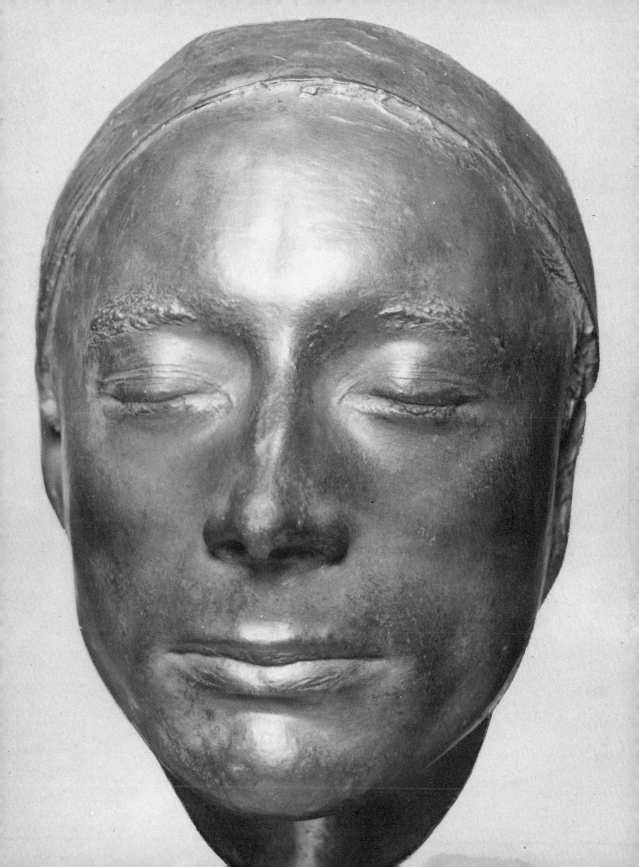

for in his book (which, incidentally, has never received the commendation it deserves) *Imagination and Fancy* he speaks with disapproval of the story that 'Boileau's trick for appearing to rhyme naturally was to compose the second line of the couplet first! which gives one the crowning idea of the "artificial school of poetry".' But at the very centre of Keats' poem are some lines that have a massive and dignified conception of poetry, one that repeats a certain Grecian note that we often find in Keats when he emerges from a copse to talk with full seriousness about his art:

> A drainless shower
> Of light is poesy; 'tis the supreme of power;
> 'Tis might half slumb'ring on its own right arm.

This last image, which with some justice has been called Michelangelesque, is soon followed by an anticipation of one of the themes of the *Ode on a Grecian Urn*, the idea that poetry

> should be a friend
> To soothe the cares, and lift the thoughts of man

—an idea far removed from the kind of self-indulgent escapism and revery with which Keats is sometimes charged.

At the same time, Keats was still serving as a part-time dresser at Guy's; his hospital life did not come to a full stop after the interview with Abbey, but continued until March 1817, when Haydon wrote in his journal, 'He has gone to dress wounds, after spending an evening with me spouting Shakespeare.'

The early nineteenth-century operating theatre of Old St Thomas' Hospital. 'Standings' for students rise around the wooden operating table and plain surgeon's chair (the more comfortable chairs were for distinguished observers); a box of sawdust under the table was moved about to catch dripping blood

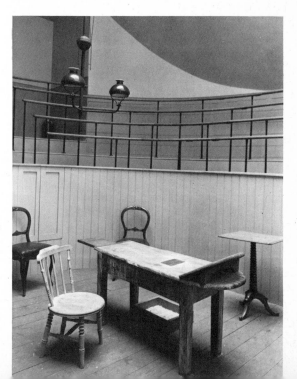

Percy Bysshe Shelley, in the Baths of Caracalla at Rome. The pose is derived from the memorial to Shakespeare in Westminster Abbey

Of the two poets with whom he was now publicly associated in Hunt's article, Keats had already met Reynolds, and had spontaneously liked him. This was not to be the case with Shelley, who began to frequent the Leigh Hunt household in the winter of 1816–17: Keats probably met him at some time during December. Shelley was famed – in circles other than Hunt's was notorious – for his attacks on Church and State. He was older than Keats; he was taller, better educated, and had a far wider range of ideas. Separated from his wife Harriet and their two children, he was now living with Mary, the daughter of the social reformer William Godwin and his wife Mary Wollstonecraft. Keats must have been struck

Shelley

35

(Left) Self-portrait of Joseph Severn at 29. When he met Keats, he wrote, 'A new world was opened to me, and I was raised from the mechanical drudgery of my art to the hope of brighter and more elevated courses.'

(Right) William Hazlitt, by William Bewick. 'The three things to rejoice at in this age', according to Keats, were Wordsworth's *Excursion*, Haydon's pictures, and 'Hazlitt's depth of taste'

by the curious combination of worldliness and innocence that characterized Shelley's publicly-led private life, no less than by the spring and daring of his conversation. He read Shelley's *Alastor* and his *Hymn to Intellectual Beauty*. Though impressed by them, he did not particularly like them. He felt an instinctive shying-away from them; and as with the poetry, so with the man. But Keats was not opposed to Shelley, nor unreceptive to him. He soon wrote a quick poem with the Shelleyan title *Written in Disgust of Vulgar Superstition*. An interest in ideas later to be nurtured by such friends as Hazlitt and Benjamin Bailey may have been first aroused by the fervent abstractions of Shelley, and *Alastor* probably contributed a little to *Endymion*.

Shelley's descent on this small and rather self-enclosed part of artistic London took some of its members by storm. Hunt, certainly, was completely overwhelmed, especially when Shelley lent him £1,500. Others, perhaps, were made to feel slightly provincial. Haydon, however, was determined not to be impressed by an atheist, and has left us an amusing account of Shelley (who was a vegetarian) at a dinner-party given by Horace Smith, a somewhat sophisticated literary host who lived in Knightsbridge. Haydon found him 'a hectic, spare, weakly yet intellectual-looking creature . . . carving a bit of broccoli or cabbage on his plate,

36

as if it had been the substantial wing of a chicken.' To the painter's shocked dismay and anger, Shelley then 'opened up the conversation by saying in the most feminine and gentle voice, "As to that detestable religion, the Christian . . .".' Keats was present at this dinner, but remained silent. He probably felt that he wanted to keep his reserve about Shelley.

As we have seen, Keats this winter was rapidly absorbed into a circle of literary and artistic people characterized by their youth, their liberal opinions, and their vivid interest – the interest of practitioners – in poetry. They were also in close contact with the visual arts. Keats had recently met Joseph Severn, the young painter who was to accompany him to Rome in a few years' time. William Hazlitt, whom he met in Haydon's studio, was a practising art critic who had begun life as a painter. Leigh Hunt was something of a connoisseur, and was a nephew of a President of the Royal Academy, Benjamin West. This circle of friends formed a welcoming party for Keats' first book when it appeared at the beginning of March *'Poems' 1817* 1817. They were alone. Dedicated to Hunt, the volume consisted of 'I stood tip-toe', the three verse letters written at Margate, seventeen sonnets, and *Sleep and Poetry*. Hindsight enables us to see the importance of these poems. But, as Charles Cowden Clarke ruefully reported, 'the book might have emerged in Timbuctoo with a far stronger chance of fame and approbation!'

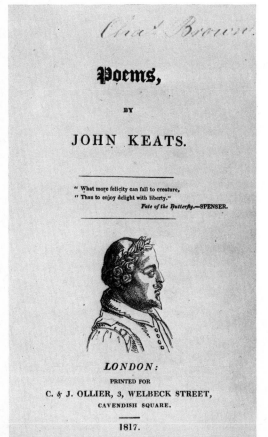

Charles Brown's copy of Keats' first book of poems. Clarke recorded that on Monday 3 March 'the first volume of Keats' minor muse was launched amid the cheers and fond anticipations of all his circle'

37

The book was unsuccessful, not because it was criticized, but because it went unnoticed. And indeed it was a trifle thin, as Keats himself was uncomfortably aware. His feelings wavered between disappointment and determination. He began to think, not that Abbey had been right, but that the confidence with which he had faced Abbey needed more substantiation. This feeling was intensified when he had the remarkable experience of a kind of admonitory and enlivening inspiration from a non-verbal art, sculpture. In the same week that the book was published Haydon took Keats with him to see the sculptures from the Parthenon. These have always been known as the Elgin Marbles, after the seventh Earl of Elgin who, while British Ambassador at Constantinople in 1801, had obtained permission from the Turkish authorities in Athens to remove them. Elgin sold the marbles to the British Government in 1816. Their genuineness, disputed by such old-fashioned connoisseurs as Richard Payne Knight (and Byron too), had been enthusiastically and vociferously upheld by Haydon, whose Romantic adulation of the classical made him their ideal cicerone, the very person to give Keats an idea of the greatness of what was probably the most important group of Greek sculptures brought to Europe. The poet's response was immediate, and vividly expressed in two poems he addressed to Haydon, who now seemed a stronger and wiser counsellor than Hunt. Behind these two sonnets, with their quite complicated emotions, lies a consciousness of Keats' own shortcomings, a determination to study and emulate greatness, and a simple wish for a new start.

The Elgin Marbles

A fragment of the Elgin Marbles:

Such dim-conceived glories of the brain
Bring round the heart an indescribable feud;
So do these wonders a most dizzy pain,
That mingles Grecian grandeur with the rude
Wasting of old Time – with a billowy main –
A sun – a shadow of a magnitude.

Keats was to remember this scene of sacrifice in the *Ode on a Grecian Urn*

The temporary Elgin Room at the British Museum in 1819. Seated in the left foreground is
Benjamin West (Leigh Hunt's uncle); Haydon is standing at the extreme left

In March 1817 the Keats brothers decided to move from Cheapside to Hampstead. The air, they may well have thought, would be better for Tom, whose health
was now a cause for real concern. They went to lodge on the first floor of the home
of the local postman, Benjamin Bentley, at No. 1 Well Walk. At about this time
Keats met, probably through Reynolds, John Taylor, who had a publishing and
bookselling business in Fleet Street. Soon his firm, Taylor and Hessey, took over
from the Ollier brothers as Keats' publishers. Taylor was quite unconcerned
about the failure of Keats' first book, and not in the slightest put off by what was
sniffily described at the time as the poet's 'singular style of dress'. He was convinced
that he had discovered a writer of rare talent, and wrote that 'I cannot think he

39

Keats' publishers were continually helpful to him, and were convinced of his talent. Taylor (*left*) wrote that 'Keats will be the brightest Ornament of his Age', and Hessey (*right*) said of Keats' last volume, 'I think no single volume of Poems ever gave me more real delight.'

will fail to become a great poet.' Encouraged by the firm's belief in his future, tangibly demonstrated by an advance of £20, Keats packed a bag, not forgetting plenty of paper and a pocket-size edition of Shakespeare, and on 14 April caught a coach to Southampton. He was going away to write, to extend himself, to see what he could do.

'*Endymion*' What exactly was this 'trial of invention', this exercise of his own powers, the poem which was to occupy him for the rest of the year? *Endymion* is Keats' attempt at a poem of epic length (of epic length rather than scope, we should note), and was largely determined by his simple conviction that great poets wrote long poems. He described his plans in a letter to George that he subsequently thought important enough to copy out for a new friend, Bailey:

> [*Endymion*] will be a test, a trial of my Powers of Imagination and chiefly of my invention which is a rare thing indeed – by which I must make 4000 Lines of one bare circumstance and fill them with Poetry; and when I consider that this is a great task, and that when done it will take me but a dozen paces towards the Temple of Fame – it makes me say – God forbid that I should be without such a task! I have heard Hunt say and may be asked – why endeavour after a long Poem? To which I should answer – Do not the Lovers of Poetry like to have a little Region to wander in where they may pick and choose, and in which

40

Thy father's court? for thou shalt hear, that I,—
Knowing by Paulina, that the oracle
Gave hope thou wast in being,—have preserv'd
Myself, to see the issue.
    Paul.   There's time enough for that;
Lest they desire, upon this push to trouble
Your joys with like relation.—Go together,
You precious winners all: your exultation
Partake to every one.   I, an old turtle,
Will wing me to some wither'd bough; and there
My mate, that's never to be found again,
Lament till I am lost.
    Leon.   O peace, Paulina;
Thou should'st a husband take by my consent,
As I by thine, a wife: this is a match,
And made between's by vows.   Thou hast found mine;
But how, is to be question'd: for I saw her,
As I thought, dead; and have, in vain, said many
A prayer upon her grave: I'll not seek far
(For him, I partly know his mind,) to find thee
An honourable husband:—Come, Camillo,
And take her by the hand: whose worth, and honesty,
Is richly noted; and here justified
By us, a pair of kings.—Let's from this place.—
What?—Look upon my brother:—both your pardons,
That e'er I put between your holy looks
My ill suspicion.—This your son-in-law,
And son unto the king, (whom heavens directing,)
Is troth-plight to your daughter.—Good Paulina,
Lead us from hence; where we may leisurely
Each one demand, and answer to his part
Perform'd in this wide gap of time, since first
We were dissever'd: Hastily lead away.   [*Exeunt.*

This play, as Dr. Warburton justly observes, is, with
all its absurdities, very entertaining. The character of
Autolycus is naturally conceived, and strongly represented.   JOHNSON.

to fool again.

A page, actual size, from the newly-bought seven-volume set of Shakespeare that Keats took with him to the Isle of Wight in 1817. Keats never appreciated Dr Johnson, on whose edition this one was based; and he used quotations from the plays themselves – in this case, Paulina's comment on Leontes – to poke fun at him

the images are so numerous that many are forgotten and found new in a second
Reading: which may be food for a Week's stroll in the Summer?

It may be noticed in this paragraph that Keats is remarkably uninsistent on the
qualities of 'nobility' and 'the strife of human hearts', which he had mentioned
in *Sleep and Poetry* as something to be ambitious for. These epic qualities are not to
be found in *Endymion*; nor, as Keats himself makes quite clear in his letter, was
any such thing intended. It seems rather that he simply wished to extend those
poetic qualities which he already possessed, and to extend them simply in terms
of length. *Endymion*, consequently, is diffuse, languid, dabbling. We will find,
however, that in the course of its composition Keats changed himself into a
different, far more mature, poet. *Endymion*, to be frank, is a bore to read; but it was
perhaps the most valuable of Keats' not infrequent attempts at education and self-
improvement, and it is impossible to comprehend the triumphs and achievements
of the later poetry, and indeed the whole question of his immensely rapid progress
towards maturity as a poet, without explaining it by the work done in these months
of 1817.

Endymion is a romance, into which we may read allegorical intentions. Such
intentions are surely to do with the subject of poetry, and with the discovery of its
mysteries by such a pilgrim in poetry's eye as Keats himself. But we should
remember that the poem is so much a *process* of self-discovery, rather than its
examination, that any such intentions – and Keats, after all, was remarkably free
of 'palpable designs' – are changeable. They transform themselves as he transformed himself. Our interpretations have to be altered continually. We should be
wary of imposing a pattern on the poem, for it is essentially fluid, the record of a
progression.

However, it is impossible not to see the basic situation of the poem, its 'one
bare circumstance', as being in some measure symbolical. As we have seen, Keats
had early on been attracted to the classical story of Endymion, and had some
intention of using it in his lines beginning 'I stood tip-toe'. In Greek myth the
shepherd boy Endymion is loved by Diana, Cynthia, the moon, and Keats would
have been familiar with the story from the kind of books of myth that he had known
as a schoolboy at Enfield – books like Lemprière's *Classical Dictionary* and Tooke's
Pantheon. Lemprière states that 'the fable of Endymion's amours with Diana, or
the moon, arises from his knowledge of astronomy, and as he passed the night on
some high mountain, to observe the heavenly bodies, it has been reported that he
was courted by the moon.' Such a figure was easily transformed into a composite
of the poet, the human imagination, or the human soul, in its search for beauty.
If this symbolism is attractive as a piece of neat meaningfulness, we should perhaps
think of the uninvolved delight which Keats took in the story itself, as he described

Diana visiting the sleeping Endymion: one of 'Tassie's gems', providing cheap reproductions of classical gems as well as seals with popular heroes on them (see Keats' Shakespeare, p. 106), which were avidly collected by Keats' friends

it in a touching elder-brotherly letter to Fanny (written on 10 September, while he was working on the third book of *Endymion*).

This letter suggests 'Perhaps you might like to know what I am writing about—I will tell you'. Keats then describes his poem as follows:

> Many Years ago there was a young handsome Shepherd who fed his flocks on a Mountain's Side called Latmus—he was a very contemplative sort of a Person and lived solitry among the trees and Plains little thinking—that such a beautiful Creature as the Moon was growing mad in Love with him—However so it was; and when he was asleep on the Grass, she used to come down from heaven and admire him excessively from a long time; and at last could not refrain from carying him away in her arms to the top of that high Mountain Latmus while he was a dreaming—but I dare say [you] have read this and all the other beautiful Tales which have come down from the ancient times of that beautiful Greece. If you have not let me know and I will tell you more at large of others quite as delightful.

While making every allowance for the fact that Keats is addressing his younger sister, still at school, we cannot help but feel from this plain and loving account of the romance that the 'meaning' is not what Keats himself found most attractive in his subject.

43

'I have not seen many specimens of Ruins – I dont think however I shall see one to surpass Carisbrooke Castle. The trench if o'ergrown with the smoothest turf, and the walls with ivy – the Keep within side is one Bower of ivy – a Colony of Jackdaws have been there many years' (Letter to Reynolds, 17 April 1817)

'I go to Canterbury – having got tired of Margate – I was not right in my head when I came – at Cant^y I hope the Remembrance of Chaucer will set me forward like a Billiard-Ball' (Letter to Taylor and Hessey, 16 May 1817)

Not, of course, that *Endymion* is without meaning; from its first line (the one that everyone remembers, 'A thing of beauty is a joy for ever') it abounds in philosophical and poetic thoughts that are more familiar to us from the great odes and the letters; though they are scarcely ever fully expressed in the same way, and lack that whole roundness, that calm, removed and unassailable quality which we find in, for instance, the *Ode on a Grecian Urn*.

From Southampton, then, with the beginnings of *Endymion* stirring in his mind, in chilly spring weather Keats crossed the Solent to the Isle of Wight and found a place to stay near Newport, within sight of the romantic outlines of Carisbrooke Castle. The landlady gave him a portrait of Shakespeare to hang in his room. Keats wanted to settle down to some work on *Endymion*, which was to occupy him for the next eight months. But he had a block; the lines would not come out, and he experienced a depressingly tense few days, sleeping badly, unable to eat. Shakespeare was a comfort, and he read him continually, echoing King Lear in a sonnet *On the Sea* written at this time. He very soon left the Isle of Wight and travelled along the coast back to Margate, familiar Margate, where he met Tom. The two brothers visited Canterbury, attracted no doubt by its medieval and Chaucerian associations.

Isle of Wight and Bo Peep

Tom went back to London and John travelled to Hastings, where he stayed for a few nights at the little resort of Bo Peep. There he had the exciting experience of

The New England Bank Inn, at Bo Peep, had probably been recommended by Haydon

(*Left*) Well Walk, leading from the Heath to the centre of the village of Hampstead. Here the Keats brothers lived together from March 1817 until George's departure for America in June 1818 and Tom's death in December of the same year

(*Right*) Hampstead Heath by Varley, looking from one of the ponds towards distant fields of wheat. The Heath and Kenwood were what remained of the ancient Forest of Middlesex; some land was cultivated, some was heathy scrub, and some was woodland

a flirtation with a somewhat enigmatic young lady, Isabella Jones. From what we know of her character she was in no sense girlish; and we know more of her accomplishments than of her exact social standing. Keats 'warmed with her . . . and kissed her', and wrote her a half-serious love poem before going back to London. The experience with Isabella Jones undoubtedly had some effect on *Endymion*. The second book of the poem opens with an encomium of the powers of romantic love, and Endymion meets an amiable nymph in a landscape that has been thought rather similar to that around Hastings.

We know that Keats had completed at least one book of his long poem when he returned to London at the beginning of the summer. Thereafter it seems to have made slow progress. There were worrying distractions. Money problems, which he had jocularly dismissed a few weeks before as 'nettles in the bed', seemed more serious. There was the question of Tom's health. And Keats was upset by something which related directly to his poetic ambitions, for both George Felton Mathew and Leigh Hunt had published disappointing reviews of his book; Mathew's had some spite in it, and Hunt's was patronizing and obtuse. 'I do not

know what has happened to Junkets,' said Hunt (using the nickname he had derived from the sound of the poet's name), 'I suppose Queen Mab has eaten him.' The reason why Hunt had not seen him is plain enough; Keats was disappointed in their friendship.

The second book of *Endymion* was written in Hampstead in the summer of 1817. He saw much of Reynolds, and they read Shakespeare together on Hampstead Heath. They also talked of love, for Reynolds was enamoured of a girl in Devon, and Keats himself certainly had some kind of amatory adventure which led to the slightly bawdy verses 'Unfelt, unheard, unseen'. That August, Keats spent hours walking over the Heath and through the surrounding countryside; one person often with him was Joseph Severn, who delighted in his company, and later recalled that 'nothing seemed to escape him, the song of a bird and the undernote of response from covert or hedge, the rustle of some animal, the changing of the green and brown lights and furtive shadows, the motions of the wind.' From the heights of the Heath they could look down on fields of wheat, and as the wind swelled over them Keats shouted 'The tide! The tide!'

47

Oxford   Towards the end of the second book of *Endymion* Keats' invention flagged: the verse begins to limp. With nearly two thousand lines behind him, he had fallen into some of his worst poeticizing. He was alone at Well Walk, for his brothers had gone away on a trip to the Continent. He willingly accepted the invitation of Benjamin Bailey to write the third book at Oxford, during the early autumn before the beginning of the Michaelmas term. Bailey was perhaps the best educated of Keats' immediate friends; he was certainly the most studious. He had gone up to Oxford to read for Holy Orders. Something of a writer himself, he was interested in philosophy, especially in Plato, and particularly appreciated those poets with a large philosophical vision – Milton, Wordsworth and Dante. Keats spent a month in Oxford, and wrote enthusiastically to Fanny on 10 September (in the letter where he had described *Endymion*) that 'This Oxford I have no doubt is the finest City in the world – it is full of old Gothic buildings – Spires – towers – Quadrangles – Cloisters Groves &c and is surrounded with more Clear streams than ever I saw together.' Bailey had rooms in Magdalen Hall, adjoining Magdalen College, looking out over the deer park and the Cherwell. Bailey and Keats worked after breakfast, Bailey at his philosophy and theology, Keats writing some fifty lines

(*Left*) Oxford from the meadows, 'surrounded with more Clear streams than ever I saw together'. Keats stayed at Magdalen Hall (*below*) with his friend Bailey (*right*), whom at one time he considered to be 'one of the noblest men alive at the present day. . . . He delights me in the Selfish and (please god) the disenterrested part of my disposition.'

Shakespeare's birthplace at Stratford-on-Avon, before it was made more 'Tudor' by
Victorian rebuilding

a day. In the afternoons they went out walking, or bathed in the Isis from a boat
they had hired. One day they went to Stratford, where they wrote their names on
the walls of Shakespeare's birthplace.

There were many such diversions. But the holiday was most important to Keats
for intellectual reasons. He read Wordsworth again, and this time discussed his
reading with someone who was interested in Wordsworthian thought. Bailey also
gave him Hazlitt's first book, the thoughtful *Principles of Human Action*, and made
him read one of his favourite authors, the seventeenth-century divine Jeremy
Taylor, whose grave and thickly studded devotional prose must have appealed
to Keats.

The month in Oxford had been so untroubled, so intellectually refreshing, that
Keats was repelled by the squabbles of his literary friends in London. He wrote
to Bailey that 'I am quite disgusted with literary Men and will never know another
except Wordsworth.' In wet October weather he shut himself away, dosed himself
with mercury to combat an infection – which may have been venereal – he had
picked up in Oxford, and continued with the fourth and final book of *Endymion*.

50

Jeremy Taylor, represented on the title-page of his *Rule and Exercises of Holy Living* (1651). Keats was introduced to Taylor's prose at Oxford; four years later, when he was dying in Rome, the anti-clerical Keats turned to Taylor for a book which would give him 'some faith – some hope – something to rest on now'

In November he had disturbing news to give Bailey: the previous month's issue of *Blackwood's Edinburgh Magazine* had appeared with an article entitled 'On the Cockney School of Poetry', anonymously contributed by the paper's editors. It consisted of a violent attack upon Leigh Hunt, asking 'How could any man of high original genius ever stoop publicly, at the present day, to dip his finger in the least of those glittering and rancid obscenities which float on the surface of Mr Hunt's Hippocrene? His poetry resembles that of a man who has kept company with kept-mistresses. His muse talks indelicately like a tea-sipping milliner girl.' More was promised in a further number, and Keats realized with some foreboding that his turn might be next.

A final burst was needed to complete *Endymion* and, as so often, Keats felt that the way to get work done was to leave town. He went to stay in a coaching inn, the Fox and Hounds at Burford Bridge, under the Surrey beauty-spot of Box Hill. From there on 22 November 1817 he wrote one of his most impressive letters, to Bailey, in which he attempted an amalgam of his own tactile, pulse-felt poetic nature with Hazlittian and Wordsworthian ideas. This is the letter in which he calls for 'a Life of Sensations rather than of Thoughts' and states that 'I am certain of nothing but of the holiness of the Heart's affections and the truth of Imagination – What the imagination seizes as Beauty must be truth.' As he came to the end of

Poetry defined

51

Burford Bridge,
with Box Hill in
the distance

Endymion–that enormous endeavour for so young and so unpractised a poet–there
are, in this letter, all the signs of a new-found calm and poetic maturity.

What goes on in *Endymion*? We have seen how the project to write such a poem
originated in the attraction of the Greek story. Keats began his poem with an
aesthetic exordium, a flourish which is then followed by a description of the sylvan
setting of the lower slopes of Mount Latmos, and of the shepherds, damsels, lambs,
priests and the like, who live there in mythic peace and harmony. These shepherds
sing a 'Hymn to Pan' which, taken separately, can be felt as a finely sustained
piece of writing, its initial vocative rising in power towards the end some seventy
lines later; in some ways it prefigures the great odes of the spring of 1819. There
follows a description of how Endymion has, in his dream (equated with a state of
vision) been dazzled by the sight of a goddess; this vision of the godlike is then
connected with poetry that deals with what Keats (discussing with Taylor some
revisions made at this point in January 1818) called 'a regular stepping of the
Imagination towards a Truth'. This letter has a direct bearing on *Endymion*. He
goes on to say, 'My having written that Argument will perhaps be of the greatest
Service to me of any thing I ever did–It set before me at once the gradations of
Happiness even like a kind of Pleasure Thermometer–and is my first Step towards
the chief Attempt in the Drama–the playing of different Natures with Joy and
Sorrow.' The end of the first book has to be interpreted–and what could be more
open to interpretation?–in the light of those unclearly formulated but emotionally
cohesive ideas.

52

The second book of *Endymion* begins with the episode that was probably coloured by his experiences at Hastings with Isabella Jones. After this glorification of the power of love – and yet love which is not consummated, and has not the immense importance that Keats always placed on 'possession' – Endymion has to embark on a search for the goddess he had seen in his dream on Mount Latmos. This is finally to lead to a meeting and possession that will make all earthly things seem as nothing. Keats' grip on the world, in fact, is liable to fly upwards towards poetry and love in such a way that different levels of experience are magnificently confused:

> *Now I have tasted her sweet soul to the core*
> *All other depths are shallow: essences,*
> *Once spiritual, are like muddy lees,*
> *Meant but to fertilize my earthly root,*
> *And make my branches lift a golden fruit*
> *Into the bloom of heaven . . .*

The third book, once again, begins as if Keats were editing *The Examiner*, and then settles into an ecstatic apostrophe of the moon. Its main action is Endymion's encounter with the god Glaucus, cursed by Circe for his love of Scylla. Black misery was Glaucus' lot, and it is for Endymion to rescue him; some of Keats' humanitarian concerns are present in this episode, which concludes with a scene in the Palace of Neptune.

Glaucus and Scylla, etched after Salvator Rosa, who was at the height of his English popularity in Keats' day

The fourth and final book of *Endymion* introduces the Indian Maid, whose 'Song to Sorrow' is well known as an extract from the poem as a whole. Her function in the scheme of the poem is to bring together human and divine love, and she is finally revealed as indistinct from the goddess for whom Endymion has so long been searching. It makes for a tolerably happy ending. But most readers will already have been baffled away from the movement of the poem—and not only from its story but also from its significance, which one can only summarize by saying that it concerns the resolution of the aesthetic and personal problems with which Keats was most concerned; the difference between action and contemplation; between a life of sensations, a full possession of this earth, and a spiritual life away from it, away to unknown regions which can perhaps be grasped by the ennobling and revealing power of poetry.

At the end of November, with *Endymion* finished at last, Keats suddenly relaxed, changed his metre and his whole tone to write the stanzas which begin

> *In a drear-nighted December,*
> *Too happy, happy tree,*
> *Thy branches ne'er remember*
> *Their green felicity:*

a poem clearly on the other side of a watershed, that belongs with the mature Keats of 1819, that is hardly recognizable as being by the same poet who, with all that gauche and bubbling eagerness, had begun *Endymion* eight months before.

Meets Wordsworth

He went back to London to find that Wordsworth was in town, staying with relatives. Haydon, who had known the revered poet for some time, was able to arrange an introduction, and the poets met in December 1817 at the house of Wordsworth's cousin-in-law, Monkhouse, near Cavendish Square. Keats recited for Wordsworth his 'Hymn to Pan', from *Endymion*. Despite the differences in age and temperament, they got on well enough, and Keats saw Wordsworth quite frequently during the older man's stay in London.

Horace Smith

William Wordsworth drawn by
Haydon in 1818, the year of the
'immortal dinner'

But he was at something of a loose end, both socially and poetically. George—
now unemployed–had gone with Tom to Teignmouth in Devon. Keats went
out a good deal. He went to dinner at Horace Smith's, but found the company
rather too smart for his tastes: 'These men say things which make one start, without
making one feel, they are are all alike; their manners are alike; they all know
fashionables; they have a mannerism in their very eating & drinking, in their mere
handling a Decanter.' Much more congenial was a group of sporting and frolic-
some young men who met to carouse in 'a sort of a Club', or the company of the
friendly family of Charles Wentworth Dilke. Dilke worked in Somerset House,
was according to Keats 'a Godwin-methodist', and had compiled a six-volume
edition of *Old English Plays*. He and an old schoolfriend, Charles Armitage

55

Charles Wentworth Dilke: 'a Man who cannot feel he has a personal identity unless he has made up his Mind about every thing. . . . Dilke will never come at a truth as long as he lives; because he is always trying at it.' (Letter to George and Georgiana Keats, 24 September 1819)

Brown, had recently built a semi-detached or duplex house called Wentworth Place, in a lane leading down from Hampstead to South End Green, at the southern edge of the Heath. Dilke, a family man, occupied the larger side of the house, and the bachelor Brown lived in the rest. The garden was shared. Keats was a frequent visitor at Wentworth Place, where in less than a year's time he was to meet Fanny Brawne.

Keats' appearance   At this stage we may pause to notice Keats' personal appearance. It comes as something of a surprise to learn that he was very short, only three-quarters of an inch over five feet tall. He often made rather sour remarks about this, and one of his earliest commendations of Fanny Brawne is that she was the same height as himself. However, we should bear in mind that the average stature of a grown man was in those days considerably shorter than today; and also that Keats, by all accounts, was physically impressive, because of his broad shoulders, his aggressive stance, his sense of physical energy, and, above all, the expression of his face. Practically everyone who knew him commented on this. His face, according to some, 'had an expression as though he had been looking on some glorious sight.' He had thick reddish-brown hair and hazel eyes, which, according to Haydon, 'had an inward look . . . like a Delphian priestess who saw visions.' When excited or moved, Keats' aspect seems to have been especially striking. Clarke

Front and back of Wentworth Place, Hampstead, built by Charles Wentworth Dilke and
Charles Brown in the winter of 1815–16. Dilke (and later the Brawnes) had the right side of the
house, entered by the central front door; Brown (and later Keats) had the left side, approached
by a door where the single-storey addition now is. The right-hand window under the porch
(*below*) was that of Keats' sitting-room

(*Left*) Miniature of Keats by Severn, exhibited – against Keats' wishes – at the Royal Academy in May 1819

(*Right*) Sketches of Keats from Haydon's diary for 1816. The smaller head shows Haydon's impulse to make Keats as Grecian as possible

recalled him on the way to meet Hunt for the first time, and said, 'The character and expression of Keats' features would arrest even the casual passenger in the street; and now they were wrought to a tone of animation that I could not but watch with interest.' George Keats said that his brother's 'open, prodigal' nature was to be clearly seen when 'John's eyes moistened, and his lip quivered at the relation of any tale of generosity, of benevolence or noble daring.' It is unfortunate that there is not a better collection of portraits of Keats. Many of them were done posthumously; perhaps the most convincing, especially in the way that they seem to capture his eagerness and intelligence, are the two profile heads by Haydon, one in pen and ink in a notebook, and the other in the crowd scene of his painting *Christ's Entry into Jerusalem.*

John Keats by B R Haydon

There was a spirit that in passing over the South seas . . . the
alveoley and fell most . . . . . . like a comet
. . . . and . . . in . . . .
taught to make its dull inhabitants comprehend the beauty of his
. . . . .

The theatre   Another of Keats' diversions at this time was the theatre; not the genteel theatre as we know it today, but the Regency type, a place of brash showiness on the stage and riotous disorder in the pit. Drury Lane was Keats' favourite theatre, for here he could see the diminutive but immensely forceful and empathic actor Edmund Kean, who excelled in Shakespearean roles. Keats saw him as Macbeth, Hamlet, and Richard III, and was immensely impressed by these performances. Keats even wrote some theatre criticism, temporarily taking Reynolds' place as a correspondent for John Scott's *Champion*, a periodical that was becoming a rival of *The Examiner*. Keats' enthusiasm for the theatre was shared by a man who had a considerable influence on him, the critic, journalist and literary man William Hazlitt, whom he first met during the winter months of 1816–17. Keats was familiar with his essays printed in the 'Round Table' pages of *The Examiner*, and had read his *Principles of Human Action* with Bailey in Oxford. Another book of Hazlitt's which impressed him was the *Characters of Shakespear's Plays*: an

Contending for one of the cheap seats
in a Regency theatre

Edmund Kean as
Richard III

annotated copy belonging to Keats has survived, and it shows how much the poet, with his instinctive feeling for Shakespeare, found himself in agreement with the critic.

'Negative Capability'

The inspired acting of Kean, Keats' reading of Hazlitt's *Characters of Shakespear's Plays*, and the ideas which germinated during the stay at Burford Bridge, all contributed to his famous theory – less a theory than a profound insight, perhaps – of 'Negative Capability', which he now described in a letter to his brothers on 21 December 1817: 'several things dovetailed in my mind, & at once it struck me, what quality went to form a Man of Achievement, especially in Literature, & which Shakespeare possessed so enormously – I mean *Negative Capability*, that is when man is capable of being in uncertainties, Mysteries, doubts, without any irritable reaching after fact & reason.' This is not merely a beautifully generous

The new Drury Lane Theatre, built in 1810–12. Charles Brown had free admission for life – awarded him when his play *Narensky* was produced there in January 1814 – in the form of a silver ticket, which he lent to Keats

aggravates the sense of sympathy in the reader, and of uncontroulable anguish in the swoln heart of Lear, is the petrifying indifference, the cold, calculating, obdurate selfishness of his daughters. His keen passions seem whetted on their stony hearts. The contrast would be too painful, the shock too great, but for the intervention of the Fool, whose well-timed levity comes in to break the continuity of feeling when it can no longer be borne, and to bring into play again the fibres of the heart just as they are growing rigid from over-strained excitement. The imagination is glad to take refuge in the half-comic, half-serious comments of the Fool, just as the mind under the extreme anguish of a surgical operation vents itself in sallies of wit. The character was also a grotesque ornament of the barbarous times, in which alone the tragic ground-work of the story could be laid. In another point of view it is indispensable, inasmuch as while it is a diversion to the too great intensity of our disgust, it carries the pathos to the highest pitch of which it is capable, by shewing the pitiable weakness of the old king's conduct and its irretrievable consequences in the most familiar point of view. Lear may well " beat at the gate which let his folly in," after, as the Fool says, " he has made his daughters his mothers." The character is

dropped in the third act to make room for the entrance of Edgar as Mad Tom, which well accords with the increasing bustle and wildness of the incidents; and nothing can be more complete than the distinction between Lear's real and Edgar's assumed madness, while the resemblance in the cause of their distresses, from the severing of the nearest ties of natural affection, keeps up a unity of interest. Shakespear's mastery over his subject, if it was not art, was owing to a knowledge of the connecting links of the passions, and their effect upon the mind, still more wonderful than any systematic adherence to rules, and that anticipated and outdid all the efforts of the most refined art, not inspired and rendered instinctive by genius.

One of the most perfect displays of dramatic power is the first interview between Lear and his daughter, after the designed affronts upon him, which till one of his knights reminds him of them, his sanguine temperament had led him to overlook. He returns with his train from hunting, and his usual impatience breaks out in his first words, " Let me not stay a jot for dinner; go, get it ready." He then encounters the faithful Kent in disguise, and retains him in his service ; and the first trial of his honest duty is to trip up the heels of the officious Steward who makes so prominent and despicable a figure

[handwritten marginal note, left:] This is almost the last observation from Mr Hazlitt. And is it really thus? Or as it has appeared to me? Does not the Fool by his very levity – nay it is not levity – give a finishing touch to the pathos; making what without him would be within our heart-reach really unfathomable. The Fool's words are merely

[handwritten marginal note, right:] the simplest translation of Poetry high as Lears – " Since my young Ladies going into France Sir, the Fool hath much pined away" × Aye. this is it – most likely H. is right throughout. yet is there not a little contradiction?

In the margins of the *Characters of Shakespear's Plays*, Keats carried on a dialogue with Hazlitt's text: 'This is almost the last observation from Mr Hazlitt. And is it really thus? Or as it has appeared to me? Does not the Fool by his very levity – nay it is not levity – give a finishing touch to the pathos; making what without him would be within our heart-reach really unfathomable. The Fool's words are merely the simplest translation of Poetry high as Lears – "Since my young Ladies going into France/Sir, the Fool hath much pined away".' Then, reading further, he finds Hazlitt expressing the same idea. 'Aye – this is it – most likely H. is right throughout. Yet is there not a little contradiction?'

apprehension of that quality in Shakespeare we often refer to, weakly, as his 'universality'; it is also eloquent of the fine largesse of Keats' own mind as he attempts to equate the poetic with the human personality, for the idea of 'Negative Capability' necessarily involves both. It is a wonderful Romantic notion; it assumes that a poet

Charles Lamb in 1819. Of himself, Lamb wrote, 'The informal habit of his mind, joined to an inveterate impediment of speech, forbade him to be an orator; and he seemed determined that no-one else should play that part when he was present.'

Charles Jeremiah Wells

is not simply a man with a gift for writing poems, but rather that the qualities associated with poetry – its intensity, concern with emotion, total eschewal of the dishonest, its measure and its liberality – are the constant attributes of the human being. No other poet makes us feel this so strongly as does Keats.

The 'immortal dinner'

Keats was at the pantomime at Drury Lane on Boxing Day, and a couple of days later, on 28 December, he went to dinner with Haydon. The painter afterwards referred to his party as 'immortal'; and so it was. Wordsworth was there, together with Monkhouse (the cousin at whose house he had met Keats); others came in later. But the star of the evening, transforming the occasion from loftiness to inspired buffoonery, was Charles Lamb, the essayist, punster, and author (with his sister Mary) of that sympathetic work the *Tales from Shakespeare*. Lamb loved drinking. They began with talk of the mighty: Shakespeare, Milton, Virgil and Homer. Wordsworth recited Milton 'with an intonation like the funeral bell of St Paul's and the music of Handel mingled'. Lamb, with his genius for irreverence, could not take this for long. He addressed Wordsworth as 'you old lake poet, you rascally poet'. He insisted on making speeches, he proposed toast after toast. Lamb and Keats agreed that Newton 'had destroyed all the poetry of the rainbow.' They then drank to 'Newton's health, and confusion to mathematics.' They drank everyone's health. A civil servant came in, and attempted to have a serious conversation with Wordsworth, but Lamb chanted 'Diddle diddle dumpling, my son John' every time he opened his mouth, waved a candle and shouted 'Do let me have another look at that gentleman's organs.' Finally, it became too much for Haydon; and 'Keats and I hurried Lamb into the painting-room, shut the door and gave way to inextinguishable laughter.' All evening Lamb could be heard struggling and laughing in the next room, calling out 'Who is that fellow? Allow me to see his organs once more.'

Keats greatly relished such evenings. We find him staying up all night to play cards, discussing with many a jest 'the derivation of the word C--t', covering his tongue with cayenne pepper the better to savour the claret that was his favourite drink, having an evening with Severn and Charles Wells (a schoolfriend of Tom's) when they improvised a concert by each pretending to be a musical instrument, drinking with actors in an ale-house at the back of Drury Lane, where he observed with approval, in a letter to his brothers written in January 1818, 'how they looked about, & chatted; how they did not care a Damn; was a great treat.'

Hazlitt's lectures

Early in 1818 Keats attended the lectures on the English poets that Hazlitt was giving in the Surrey Institution, just to the south of Blackfriars Bridge. There was a remarkable unanimity of feeling in the two men. For instance 'gusto', the cornerstone of Hazlitt's somewhat unsystematic thinking about painting, is quite closely paralleled in Keats' attitude to the theatre and in his reaction to Benjamin

Death on the Pale Horse. Benjamin West's famous picture, on which he had been engaged for many years, was disliked by Hazlitt as well as by Keats

West's *Death on the Pale Horse*, which he had seen in December: about it he felt 'there is nothing to be intense upon; no women one feels mad to kiss; no face swelling into reality. the excellence of every art is its intensity, capable of making all disagreeables evaporate, from their being in close relationship with Beauty & Truth.' Keats only missed one of Hazlitt's course of lectures; at that which dealt with Shakespeare and Milton he would have been particularly taken with the idea that Shakespeare was 'the least of an egoist that it was possible to be. He was nothing in himself; but was all that others were, or that they could become.'

Richard Woodhouse   Richard Woodhouse, the legal and literary adviser to the firm of Taylor and Hessey, shows himself as a particularly sensitive interpreter of Keats' mind when recording his conversations with the poet. Keats, mulling over a number of ideas this winter, obviously discussed them with his friends at some length. Woodhouse caught them neatly, and wrote them down. He describes Keats' feeling about imaginative identification with the empirical world, and says that he 'affirmed that he can conceive of a billiard ball, that it may have a sense of delight from its own roundness, smoothness volubility and the rapidity of its motion.' And in more general terms, coming back once more to Shakespeare, Woodhouse explains how the poet 'will speak out of that object – so that his own self will with the exception of the mechanical part be "annihilated" – and it is of the excess of this power that

66

The Surrey Institution, where
Hazlitt gave his course of lectures on
the English poets

Richard Woodhouse as a child. He
was the first person to make a
systematic collection of Keatsiana

67

The Enchanted Castle, by Claude Lorrain. In the verse letter which he wrote on 25 March 1818 to amuse the sick Reynolds, Keats lovingly and at length describes this, one of his favourite pictures:

> *You know the Enchanted Castle it doth stand*
> *Upon a Rock on the Border of a Lake*
> *Nested in Trees, which all do seem to shake*
> *From some old magic like Urganda's sword. . . .*
> *   You know it well enough, where it doth seem*
> *A mossy place, a Merlin's Hall, a dream.*
> *You know the clear lake, and the little Isles,*
> *The mountains blue, and cold near neighbour rills . . .*

Teignmouth, Devon, in 1818; the village lies on the right, at the mouth of the river Teign

I suppose Keats to speak, when he says he has no identity – As a poet, and when the fit is on him this is true . . . Shakespeare was a poet of the kind above mentioned – and he was perhaps the only one besides Keats who possessed this power in an extraordinary degree.' The development of such ideas is part of intellectual history, no doubt; but we can remark here that Woodhouse obviously felt them to be more a part of Keats himself than of his poetry: it is another example of the remark-able effect that Keats had on all who met him.

Keats was not in fact writing poetry in any concentrated way during these winter months. He wrote some light verse, sonnets, lyrics, and an ode *On seeing a Lock of Milton's Hair* (which Hunt showed him). The *Lines on the Mermaid Tavern* were written after a visit there in the company of Horace Smith. The light-hearted *Robin Hood* was in reply to some verses on the same subject sent to him by Reynolds. At the beginning of February 1818 he sat down with Hunt and Shelley to a sonnet competition, a form of domestic amusement much favoured by Hunt. The subject was 'The Nile'. Shelley produced his *Ozymandias*, that popular dramatiza-tion of the theme of mutability, Hunt stayed up all night to write one of his better poems, but Keats, bored with the proceedings, could only offer a somewhat stiff-jointed and mechanical poem. In these weeks he was revising proofs of *Endymion*, and one letter, written to cheer Reynolds who was ill in bed, reminds us of his total mastery of this most informal and friendly of literary forms.

The winter had been a varied one; we trace it through social occasions and occasional verse. Family problems now obtruded. Tom had spat blood. George and Tom had been in Devon, at Teignmouth, where there was congenial com-pany and a doctor who specialized in consumption. Keats went down there too at the beginning of March, in a thunderstorm. The weather was bad, and remained bad. 'You may say what you will of devonshire', he wrote to Bailey: the truth is, 'it is a splashy, rainy, misty, snowy, foggy, haily, floody, muddy, slipshod county

Teignmouth

. . . the Primroses are out, but then you are in.' He went to the theatre, where he 'got insulted, which I ought to remember to forget to tell any Body; for I did not fight.'

He looked after Tom, continued working on the proofs of *Endymion*, and wrote a preface for it. This preface gave a certain amount of trouble, and both Taylor and Reynolds felt, quite rightly, that there was something wrong with Keats' first attempt to introduce his poem. Reynolds said that it was 'affected', and indeed there was a certain false jauntiness in the tone. The easy smartness of such remarks as 'I have written to please myself, and in hopes to please others, and for love of fame; if I neither please myself, nor others, nor get fame, of what consequence is Phraseology?' obviously had to be excised. Keats was probably a trifle hurt by the bluntness with which Reynolds criticized his preface, but he tried again, and wrote the short piece that was published with the poem. It is a much better effort, and forestalls the anticipated criticisms of the literary establishment with some lines that (apart from reminding us what fine prose Keats was able to write, and making us wish that there was more of it) have a sensible attitude to the products of his poetic adolescence:

> The imagination of a boy is healthy, and the mature imagination of a man is healthy; but there is a space of life between, in which the soul is in a ferment, the character undecided, the way of life uncertain, the ambition thick-sighted: thence proceeds mawkishness, and all the thousand bitters which those men I speak of must necessarily taste in going over the following pages.

On Easter Monday Keats went to Dawlish Fair, but this was a rare diversion. Most of the time he spent indoors, reading and studying Milton, and before going back to London in May he had written *Isabella; or, The Pot of Basil*, a romance which had been in his mind for some time, probably since he had heard Hazlitt say that a contemporary verse treatment of Boccaccio's tales would no doubt be very popular. He had also discussed the idea with Reynolds; at one time the friends were thinking of jointly producing a book of narrative poems based on stories from the *Decameron*. Keats would also not have been unaware of the large sums of money that could accrue from a best-selling poem.

Keats' version differs in some important respects from the original in Italian. First of all, he had read the story in the translation by John Florio which was first published in 1620, and in this the love of Lorenzo and Isabella is given a far more romantic, idealized and sentimental treatment. Keats' version is one that concentrates on young love, the theme that he was to pursue in *The Eve of St Agnes* and *Lamia*, and in contrast with these two later poems *Isabella* certainly seems a trifle over-sentimental, despite the violence of the main action of the poem – the cruel murder of Lorenzo by Isabella's brothers – and a certain briskness (not totally sustained) in the narration.

70

Silhouettes of Georgiana and George Keats, cut in America

Keats, oddly, seems to have been unmoved by *Isabella*. He did not talk about it when writing it, which was unusual, and he hardly ever referred to it afterwards without distaste. Perhaps it was associated in his mind not only with poetic failings –for it was a poem he began without ambition–but also with his generally depressing Devonshire holiday; for it was here that he learnt George was going to marry Georgiana Wylie, the daughter of an infantry officer, and that his intentions were to emigrate to the United States.

Back in London that May Keats wrote to Bailey in a mood of dull despondency: 'I feel no spur at my Brothers going to America and am almost stony-hearted about his wedding.' He was depressed by the thought of losing George–America always seemed to Keats a very wild and vicious place–no less than by the prospect of Tom's death. A month later he wrote to Bailey, 'I have two Brothers one is driven by the "burden of society" to America the other, with an exquisite love of Life, is in a lingering state.' Only one thing seems to have lifted his spirits: a feeling for the spring. On May Day he wrote the *Ode to Maia*, a sonnet-length fragment with irregular lines, buoyant in its octet, calm in the sestet, and in some ways anticipatory of the verse structure of the great odes that were to be written a year later.

Route of Keats' and Brown's walk. Starting from Lancaster on 25 June 1818, they walked through the Lake District and passed through Dumfries before crossing briefly to northern Ireland on 6 July; back in Scotland, they explored Robert Burns' country around the rivers Ayr and Doon, then continued north into the Highlands and Hebrides, finishing in Inverness on 6 August. In 42 days they had walked 642 miles

Keats wanted to travel. He had meant to go on his brothers' Continental trip. He felt that it would be good for his poetry, and not a bad way of life, to 'put a knapsack at my back and make a pedestrian tour through the North of England, and part of Scotland—to make a sort of Prologue to the Life I intend to pursue—that is to write, to study and to see all Europe at the lowest expence.' He was think/ing quite hard about the ways in which he might be able to gain in personal and poetic experience, and at about this time he often expresses these ambitions as being interrelated, and as having something to do with rather more vaguely formulated humanitarian concerns. To Taylor he remarked, in April, 'I know nothing I have read nothing and I mean to follow Solomon's directions of "get wisdom—get understanding"—I find cavalier days are gone by. I find that I can have no enjoyment in the World but continual drinking of Knowledge—I find there is no worthy pursuit but the idea of doing some good for the world.'

It was decided that he would go with George and Georgiana to see them on the boat at Liverpool, and then set off from there on his walking tour with Charles Brown. The walking tour was to be, in some way, a deliberate exercise in the acquisition of knowledge and experience. It was the sort of thing that Hunt would never dream of doing. It was something that would help him to get out of being a 'Cockney poet'. It was a good thing to have a plan, and one that combined a holiday with a potential enlargement of his poetry; but the general prospect of George's departure was so dispiriting that, for instance, he hardly noticed the publication of *Endymion*.

George was to sail from Liverpool at the end of June. Together with Charles Brown, who had let his side of Wentworth Place, they all went to Liverpool, the newly/weds with their luggage, Keats and Brown with their knapsacks and stout shoes. The brothers made their farewells, and Keats and Brown took a coach to Lancaster. The next day they were on the road that led towards the Lakes. Just above Bowness, looking down on Windermere, Brown recalled that 'we both simultaneously came to a full stop. The lake lay before us. His bright eyes darted upon a mountain peak, beneath which was gently floating a silver cloud; thence to a very small island, adorned with the foliage of trees, that lay beneath us, and surrounded by water of a glorious hue, when he exclaimed "How can I believe in that?—surely it cannot be!"'

The walking tour

They stayed the night in the Salutation Inn at Ambleside. After 'a monstrous breakfast' Keats was anxious to pay his respects to Wordsworth, who lived nearby. But the great man was out. He was—*quantum mutatus ab illo Hectore*—busy with some local Tory electioneering. Keats wrote a note, propped it above a picture in the hall, and they went on, along Rydal Water to Grasmere and thence to Keswick. After Wordsworth's death, it was noticed that the book of Keats' poems in his library had most of its pages uncut.

Skiddaw, by Constable; Keats climbed it on 29 June. 'I have an amazing partiality for mountains in the clouds.' (*Below*) The view from above Bowness, 'turning down to which place there burst upon us the most beautiful and rich view of Winander mere and the surrounding Mountains – we dined at Bownes on Trout which I took an oar to fetch'

Charles Armitage Brown, Keats'
closest friend

The market place at Ambleside

Keats and Brown walked all the way round Derwentwater, and went to see the Falls of Lodore – before he was in the Lakes, Keats had never seen a waterfall. They climbed Skiddaw, they stayed in an inn where there was country dancing, they pushed on to Carlisle and Scotland.

Keats had been delighted with the Lake District. He was unprepared for the grimness of Scotland. They went to visit the burial-place of Robert Burns at Dumfries. Keats' sonnet written there is influenced by the freezing hell described by Dante – whose works, in Henry Francis Cary's translation, were his main reading on this holiday. The miserable nature of Scotland, that country of cold thin rain, disturbed Keats. He felt that its Calvinism was the enemy of warm human emotions: 'These kirkmen have done Scotland harm – they have banished

Grey Friars' churchyard, Dumfries. 'Burns' tomb is in the Churchyard corner, not very much to my taste, though on a scale large enough to show they wanted to honour him.'

Part of a letter to Keats' brother Tom, headed 'Cairn-something, July 17th 1818' and including a sketch of Loch Lomond

puns and laughing and kissing.' This led him to the original theory that Burns was not a real Scotsman. 'Poor unfortunate fellow—' he wrote, 'his disposition was southern.' As they went further away from England the country became harsher, and they stayed in places where no English was spoken. From Stranraer they decided to go across to Ireland. Keats had seen poverty in London; he knew what that was like. He was shocked by the poverty of rural Scotland, and even more so by that in Ulster. 'A Scotch cottage . . . is a pallace to an irish one', he wrote. They soon came back from Ireland, and proceeded to the Western Highlands, to Iona and Fort William. They climbed Ben Nevis, which was an unpleasant experience, and Keats wrote a sonnet on the top. But the hard weather was becoming too much for him. He saw a doctor in Inverness, who advised him to go home at once.

Maria Dilke, the wife of
Charles Wentworth Dilke

When Keats got back to London in the middle of August, having travelled by boat from Cromarty, he burst into Wentworth Place to see the Dilkes. Mrs Dilke, that amiable, motherly young woman, clucked, 'he was as brown and as shabby as you can imagine; scarcely any shoes left, his jacket all torn at the back, a fur cap, a great plaid, and his knapsack, I cannot tell what he looked like.' The Dilkes had to break the news to him that Tom had entered the final stages of his illness. He left immediately and rushed up to Well Walk – without meeting the Brawne family, who had rented Brown's side of the house.

Tom's illness   There now began a period in Keats' life when he was shut away with Tom in the most harrowing and hopeless of circumstances. With George gone, the two brothers would naturally have become even closer to each other, and their quiet life together now, hardly ever moving from the house, is made all the more poignant by the fact that Tom was dying. They saw no one; so enclosed were they that the

A note in Keats' copy of *King Lear*, which he was reading by the bedside of his dying
brother Tom

'd | Too little care of this: Take Physicke, Pompe,
:e | Expose thy selfe to feele what wretches feele,
   | That thou maist shake the superflux to them,
   | And shew the Heauens more iust.

e- |
ie | *Enter Edgar, and Foole.*
1, |
ie | *Edg.* Fathom, and halfe, Fathom and halfe; poore *Tom*.   ✗ Sunday Evening
of | *Foole.* Come not in heere Nuncle, here's a spirit, helpe   Oct. 4. 1818–
I | me, helpe me.
d | *Kent.* Giue me thy hand, who's there?
of | *Foole.* A spirite, a spirite, he sayes his name's poore
:o | *Tom*.
g | *Kent.* What art thou that dost grumble there i'th'
rs | straw? Come forth.

to his succession, the greater seems to be the impulse to hasten the return of similar embarrassments,—a prepossession for which I confess myself unable to account satisfactorily, unless by admitting the force of habit, which we all know " is prodigious and unaccountable."

Should you, Mr Editor, consider this sketch worthy of appearing in print, it may, however slight, afford a cud for rumination to some of your readers, and may perhaps induce me, in a future Number, to consider, a little more at large, a subject which I have only touched		SKIN DEEP.

COCKNEY SCHOOL OF POETRY.

No IV.

———— OF KEATS,
THE MUSES' SON OF PROMISE, AND WHAT FEATS
HE YET MAY DO, &c.
					CORNELIUS WEBB.

OF all the manias of this mad age, the most incurable, as well as the most common, seems to be no other than the *Metromanie*. The just celebrity of Robert Burns and Miss Baillie has had the melancholy effect of turning the heads of we know not how many farm-servants and unmarried ladies; our very footmen compose tragedies, and there is scarcely a superannuated governess in the island that does not leave a roll of lyrics behind her in her band-box. To witness the disease of any human understanding, however feeble, is distressing; but the spectacle of an able mind reduced to a state of insanity is of course ten times more afflicting. It is with such sorrow as this that we have contemplated the case of Mr John Keats. This young man appears to have received from nature talents of an excellent, perhaps even of a superior order—talents which, devoted to the purposes of any useful profession, must have rendered him a respectable, if not an eminent citizen. His friends, we understand, destined him to the career of medicine, and he was bound apprentice some years ago to a worthy apothecary in town. But all has been undone by a sudden attack of the malady to which we have alluded. Whether Mr John had been sent home with a diuretic or composing draught to some patient far gone in the poetical mania, we have not heard. This much is certain, that he has caught the infection, and that thoroughly. For some time we were in hopes, that he might get off with a violent fit or two; but of late the symptoms are terrible. The phrenzy of the " Poems" was bad enough in its way; but it did not alarm us half so seriously as the calm, settled, imperturbable drivelling idiocy of " Endymion." We hope, however, that in so young a person, and with a constitution originally so good, even now the disease is not utterly incurable. Time, firm treatment, and rational restraint, do much for many apparently hopeless invalids; and if Mr Keats should happen, at some interval of reason, to cast his eye upon our pages, he may perhaps be convinced of the existence of his malady, which, in such cases, is often all that is necessary to put the patient in a fair way of being cured.

The readers of the Examiner newspaper were informed, some time ago, by a solemn paragraph, in Mr Hunt's best style, of the appearance of two new stars of glorious magnitude and splendour in the poetical horizon of the land of Cockaigne. One of these turned out, by and by, to be no other than Mr John Keats. This precocious adulation confirmed the wavering apprentice in his desire to quit the gallipots, and at the same time excited in his too susceptible mind a fatal admiration for the character and talents of the most worthless and affected of all the versifiers of our time. One of his first productions was the following sonnet, " *written on the day when Mr Leigh Hunt left prison.*" It will be recollected, that the cause of Hunt's confinement was a series of libels against his sovereign, and that its fruit was the odious and incestuous " Story of Rimini."

" What though, for shewing truth to flattered state,
	Kind Hunt was shut in prison, yet has he,
	In his immortal spirit been as free
As the sky-searching lark, and as elate.
Minion of grandeur! think you he did wait?
	Think you he nought but prison walls did see,
	Till, so unwilling, thou unturn'dst the key?
Ah, no! far happier, nobler was his fate!
In Spenser's halls! he strayed, and bowers fair,
	Culling enchanted flowers; and he flew

The first page of *Blackwood's* attack on Keats, August 1818

Dilkes, their near neighbours and friends, assumed that they were out of town. And, apart from the Dilke family, there was no one who was in any sense *in loco parentis* to the two boys. There was Abbey, of course, their guardian; but neither of them wanted to see him; he would have been no help. He disapproved of the Keats family, felt that there was bad blood in them, kept Fanny away from her brothers as much as he could, and had been gratuitously insulting about Keats' book when given a copy, actually telling its young author that 'Your book is hard to understand and good for nothing when it is understood.'

'Blackwood's' attack Keats was ill himself, and had to keep dosing himself with various medicines. The expedition to Scotland had been too much of a strain. He would now have another reason to dislike the country, for from Edinburgh came the long-expected attack from *Blackwood's*, which sneered at his medical training and ended: 'It is a better and a wiser thing to be a starved apothecary than a starved poet; so back to the shop Mr John, back to the "plasters, pills and ointment boxes", etc. But, for heaven's sake, young Sangrado, be a little more sparing of extenuatives and soporifics in your practice than you have been in your poetry.' This was an immensely galling thing for a young man who was using his medical knowledge to ease the pains of a loved brother, now almost past the aid of medicine.

In the middle of September, however, when Keats went to a small party given by his publishers, he was in quite good form. Hazlitt was there. The critic had been attacked in the same number of *Blackwood's*, and had fought back hard, starting legal action against the editors who, rattled, quickly settled out of court. Hessey noted that Keats 'seems altogether more rational than usual – but he is such a man of fits and starts he is not much to be depended on. Still he thinks of nothing but poetry as his being's end and aim, and some time or other he will, I doubt not, do something valuable.'

At much the same time as this party, when it must have been heartening to see Hazlitt, Keats called on the Reynolds family, and was introduced to Reynolds' cousin, Jane Cox. He thought she was splendid. 'She is not a Cleopatra,' he said, mixing a kind of reserve with wild praise, 'but she is at least a Charmian. She has a rich eastern look; she has fine eyes and fine manners. When she comes into a room she makes an impression the same as the Beauty of a Leopardess.' This was to George, in October. He had also written to Reynolds about his cousin, but without saying who she was:

I never was in love – Yet the voice and the shape of a woman has haunted me these two days – at such a time when the relief, the feverous relief of Poetry seems a much less crime – This morning Poetry has conquered – I have relapsed into those abstractions which are my only life – I feel escaped from a new strange and threatening sorrow. – And I am thankful for it – There is an awful warmth

A page (actual size) from the copy of Dante's
Inferno which Keats took on his northern holiday.
Certain of the underlined passages suggest
Hyperion, then germinating in Keats' mind;
others seem to prefigure the *Ode to a Nightingale*,
written in 1819

about my heart like a load of Immortality. Poor Tom – that woman – and Poetry
were ringing changes in my senses.

A new note is struck in this letter; we feel that Keats has deepened his responses *'Hyperion'*
to the world, and the poetry which now emerges is stronger and more serious than
any written before. As we read the first lines of *Hyperion*,

> Deep in the shady sadness of a vale
> Far sunken from the healthy breath of morn,
> Far from the fiery noon, and eve's one star,
> Sat gray-hair'd Saturn, quiet as a stone,

we are aware of a tone that has never been heard in Keats' poetry. Indeed, the lines
might be by a different poet altogether. During the next twelve months, Keats was
to write some of the greatest poems in the English language.

We have already seen Keats' ambitions for a *lengthy* poem, how he fulfilled most
of them in writing *Endymion*, and have noted that these ambitions were essentially

different from a concern with epic. Now, we find that in *Hyperion* he makes a considerable contribution to the history of the English epic tradition. He himself was well aware of this, for to Haydon he wrote of his poem that

> the nature of *Hyperion* will lead me to treat it in a more naked and grecian Manner—and the march of passion and endeavour will be undeviating—and one great contrast between them [he is thinking of *Endymion* here] will be—that the Hero of the written tale being mortal is led on, like Buonaparte, by circumstance; whereas the Apollo in Hyperion being a fore-seeing God will shape his actions like one.

The major English poets all made their attempt at epic, usually in a form that does not quite approximate to the classical models of Virgil and Homer, but is to some extent inspired by them, and is modified by the local traditions and specific-ally English concerns of our own national poetry. Spenser's *Faerie Queene* is some-thing of an epic, and Shakespeare comes close to the genre in his historical tetralogy that ends with the triumph of Henry V. Milton is the English poet most concerned with epic poetry, and in some ways he comes nearest to its classical models. The eighteenth century translated epics, or produced mock-epics. Wordsworth internal-ized the form in *The Prelude*, which was to be part of a yet wider design. In the nineteenth century Ruskin used a sweeping sense of cultural history to write what is essentially an epic (as its Miltonic first sentence immediately indicates), *The Stones of Venice*; and an epic sense of civilization, in our own century, lies behind T. S. Eliot's *The Waste Land*.

To mention such examples is to invoke the highest standards of literary greatness, and Keats' contribution to this tradition is one indication of his stature as a major English writer—a position he holds not only as the author of some few famous odes and a lyric or two, but also as a man whose thoughtful, deliberate and majestic production in *Hyperion* so clearly marks him as a central figure in the course of English poetry. For one remarkable quality of *Hyperion* is the way in which Keats assimilates the multiplicity of its literary forefathers—of whom Milton is the greatest and the most pervasive—and produces verse that is totally his own, and can hardly be described by the usual analyses of derivation. Apart from Milton, there are reminiscences of Spenser, Shakespeare and Chapman, of English versions of Homer and Hesiod, and of a number of Renaissance and eighteenth-century

Keats' copy of Milton's *Paradise Lost*. At the opening of Book IV he writes: 'A friend of mine ▶ says this Book has the finest opening of any – the point of time is gigantically critical – the wax is melted, the seal is about to be applied – and Milton breaks out "*O for that warning voice &c*". There is moreover an opportunity for a Grandeur of Tenderness–the opportunity is not lost. Nothing can be higher–Nothing so more than delphic–'

A friend of mine says this Book has the finest
opening of any - the point of time is again
really critical - 85 the war is melted. the
seal is about to bee applied - and Milt
breaks out " O for that warning voice"
Ther is moreover an opportunity for a
Grandeur of Tenderness. the opportunity
is not lost. nothing can be higher - nothing
is more than delphic -

PARADISE LOST.

BOOK IV.

O FOR that warning voice, which he who saw
The Apocalypse heard cry in Heaven aloud,
Then when the Dragon, put to second rout,
Came furious down to be revenged on men,
"Woe to the inhabitants on earth!" that now,   5
While time was, our first parents had been warn'd
The coming of their secret foe, and 'scaped,
Haply so 'scaped his mortal snare : for now
Satan, now first inflamed with rage, came down,
The tempter ere the accuser of mankind,   10
To wreck on innocent frail man his loss
Of that first battle, and his flight to Hell :
Yet not rejoicing in his speed, though bold
Far off and fearless, nor with cause to boast,
Begins his dire attempt, which, nigh the birth, 15
Now rolling boils in his tumultuous breast,
And like a devilish engine back recoils
Upon himself ; horror and doubt distract
His troubled thoughts, and from the bottom stir
The Hell within him ; for within him Hell   20
He brings, and round about him, nor from Hell
One step no more than from himself can fly

writers. It is a literary epic, in many ways; but it does not depend on literariness (which is to make a sharp distinction from eighteenth-century epic productions), and to dig inspirations out of the rich soil of *Hyperion*'s verse is usually to damage its effect, not to illuminate it.

The meaning of *Hyperion* cannot be other than obscure, since the poem is unfinished and since Keats, in a real sense, did not quite know what he was writing. Apollo's great speech, he told Woodhouse, was hardly 'composed', but 'seemed to come by chance or magic—to be as it were something given to him.' But it has always seemed most natural to think of the poem as a continuation and rewriting of the theme of *Endymion* now transposed to a godlike level. It is heroically serious. The first book opens in a deeply hushed stillness, after the war between the old Titans and the new gods, and its immense gravity makes all the more potent the discussions between Saturn, Hyperion, Thea, Coelius and Oceanus, which we must feel as the appropriate introductions to that speech of Apollo's in the third book which seems to summarize all that Keats himself had ever felt of the power of poetry—and all that he ever would feel:

'Knowledge enormous makes a God of me.
'Names, deeds, gray legends, dire events, rebellions,
'Majesties, sovran voices, agonies,
'Creations and destroyings, all at once
'Pour into the wide hollows of my brain,
'And deify me, as if some blythe wine
'Or bright elixir peerless I had drunk,
'And so become immortal.'

There is in *Hyperion*—Apollo's speech is the most obvious example of it—a sort of calm *superbia* or pride that continually insists not so much on the translatable and summarizable content of the poem as on its own strength. Its heroism makes it one of the most massively felt of English poems. It has an almost awe-inspiring grandeur, in its knowledge of Titans, as it slowly flexes its huge muscles, moves like a mountain, and rises above the repose of its forests. Here indeed is what Keats had sensed, not only in his vision of poetry, but in himself, a few months before, 'might half-slumb'ring on its own right arm'.

Hyperion was so different from *Endymion*, and so confident was he now, that further attacks on that epic of apprenticeship meant nothing to him. He realized that the writing of *Endymion* had matured him, and wrote to Hessey in October that 'In Endymion, I leaped headlong into the Sea, and thereby have become better acquainted with the Soundings, the quicksands, & the rocks, than if I had stayed upon the green shore, and piped a silly pipe, and took tea & comfortable advice.' The effort of writing it—and, to some extent, of revising it—contributed to the

Fingal's Cave, Staffa, which Keats saw on 24 July, and remembered when he began *Hyperion*: 'Suppose now the Giants who rebelled against Jove had taken a whole Mass of black Columns and bound them together like bunches of matches – and then with immense Axes had made a cavern in the body of these columns . . . such as fingal's Cave'

remarkably adult temper of his mind. He cared little for the attacks of John Wilson Croker in *The Quarterly Review*, and said, 'I think I shall be among the English poets after my death.'

In view of the fact that it was long believed during the nineteenth century that *The critics* Keats was practically brought to his grave by the criticisms of the reviewers, it is as well to notice that the young poet was relatively untroubled by them: he had other things to get on with. As a matter of fact, it is probably true to say that he was usually more upset by chance remarks about his poetry made by his friends than by anything the journalists could say about him. Reviewing generally was in a poor state, and could not be highly regarded either by authors or by potential readers. Anonymous reviewing was sometimes held to be responsible for this state of affairs, and was vehemently attacked by, among others, Bulwer Lytton,

Egyptian art and antiquities; and we trust that every possible encouragement will be given to those exertions by rewarding him liberally for what he has done, and by promises of future rewards proportioned to the value of his discoveries; for if we are rightly informed, he is not in circumstances to incur expense without the chance of remuneration.

ART. VII.—*Endymion: A Poetic Romance.* By John Keats. London. 1818. pp. 207.

REVIEWERS have been sometimes accused of not reading the works which they affected to criticise. On the present occasion we shall anticipate the author's complaint, and honestly confess that we have not read his work. Not that we have been wanting in our duty—far from it—indeed, we have made efforts almost as super-human as the story itself appears to be, to get through it; but with the fullest stretch of our perseverance, we are forced to confess that we have not been able to struggle beyond the first of the four books of which this Poetic Romance consists. We should extremely lament this want of energy, or whatever it may be, on our parts, were it not for one consolation—namely, that we are no better acquainted with the meaning of the book through which we have so painfully toiled, than we are with that of the three which we have not looked into.

It is not that Mr. Keats, (if that be his real name, for we almost doubt that any man in his senses would put his real name to such a rhapsody,) it is not, we say, that the author has not powers of language, rays of fancy, and gleams of genius—he has all these; but he is unhappily a disciple of the new school of what has been somewhere called Cockney poetry; which may be defined to consist of the most incongruous ideas in the most uncouth language.

Of this school, Mr. Leigh Hunt, as we observed in a former Number, aspires to be the hierophant. Our readers will recollect the pleasant recipes for harmonious and sublime poetry which he gave us in his preface to ' Rimini,' and the still more facetious instances of his harmony and sublimity in the verses themselves; and they will recollect above all the contempt of Pope, Johnson, and such like poetasters and pseudo-critics, which so forcibly contrasted itself with Mr. Leigh Hunt's self-complacent approbation of

——— ' all

The beginning of John Wilson Croker's review of Endymion in *The Quarterly Review*, which appeared in September 1818

This is none of my doing. I was ill at the time. 'This is a lie.' Keats' comments on the note Taylor had printed at the opening of *Lamia*. (The page was trimmed in a later rebinding)

in his *England and the English*. Despite widespread dissatisfaction, standards did not improve, and were not to do so for another fifteen or twenty years. Meanwhile Keats, like many another writer, had simply to ride the punches of *Blackwood's*, of *The Quarterly Review* and of *The British Critic*, which echoed *Blackwood's* earlier suggestion that Hunt's poetry was in some ways sexually immoral: 'We will not disgust our readers by retailing to them the artifices of vicious refinement, by which, under the semblance of "slippery blisses, twinkling eyes, soft complexion of faces, and smooth excess of hands", he would palm upon the unsuspicious and the innocent, imaginations better adapted to the stews.'

making clothes; she quite enjoyed reading, but preferred 'diverting' books. When she left school, she was soon introduced to the more gay and fashionable sides of Hampstead life: meeting the officers from the barracks in St John's Wood, going to the newly opened assembly rooms in Holly Hill, finding a welcome in the eighteenth-century houses – in one of which Sarah Siddons had lived – at the top of Windmill Hill, where the Heath begins. She knew this type of society well. It must have been agreeable to meet a poet too, even a poet as weighed down with worry as Keats.

Death of Tom   Tom was barely nineteen when he died, on the morning of 1 December 1818. Keats had hardly left his side for weeks beforehand. Now, before breakfast-time, he walked out of the house in Well Walk, went down the hill to Wentworth Place and let himself in through the side door that was used as an entrance to Brown's part of the house. Brown later wrote, 'I was awakened in my bed by a pressure on my hand. It was Keats, who came to tell me that his brother was no more.'

Brown suggested that Keats should come to live with him, and the poet soon moved down to live in Wentworth Place. Bentley, the friendly postman, carried his books down in a laundry-basket. He had few other possessions. Everyone helped; and the general feeling among Keats' friends seems to have been that they should take him out and amuse him. They went to see Kean in a new tragedy

(*Left*) The 'Gate of Judgement' at St Stephen's, Coleman Street, commemorating the Great Plague of 1665. Through it Keats followed his father and mother and finally, in December 1818, his brother Tom, to burial in the church beyond

(*Right*) Keats in his sitting room at Wentworth Place (see p. 57). Painted by Severn in Rome in 1821, after the poet's death, the picture probably records a characteristic pose. Note the portrait of Shakespeare on the wall

Fanny Brawne: a miniature painted in 1833 just after her marriage to Louis Lindon. 'Shall I
give you Miss Brawn?' wrote Keats to Georgiana and George on 18 December 1818; 'She is
about my height – with a fine style of countenance of the lengthen'd sort – she wants sentiment in
every feature – she manages to make her hair look well – her nostrils are fine – though a little
painful – her mouth is bad and good – her Profil is better than her full-face which indeed is not
full but pale and thin without showing any bone'

92

Costume sketches in a letter from Fanny Brawne to Fanny Keats, July 1822. She began writing
to Keats' sister, at his request, when he left for Italy in September 1820

at Drury Lane, and joined the bibulous and gambling crowds that left town to
go to see a prize-fight in Sussex. Keats visited his sister Fanny. He had to see Abbey.
Apart from this, he was taken to call on a variety of people, most of them friends,
others not. With Hunt, he went to a party given by the composer Vincent Novello,
which he found sickening.

As the first shock of Tom's death wore off, he was able to write to George and
Georgiana. This letter, begun on 16 December, contains his first reference to
Fanny Brawne. He says: 'Mrs Brawne who took Brown's house for the Summer, *Fanny Brawne*
still resides in Hampstead – she is a very nice woman – and her daughter senior is
I think beautiful and elegant, graceful, silly, fashionable and strange we have a
little tiff now and then – and she behaves a little better, or I must have sheered off.'
'Fashionable' Fanny certainly was; she cared for nothing so much as she cared for
clothes, even keeping careful scrapbooks of historical costume. She made the best

93

of herself; she was certainly charming, and was probably a little vexing too. We do not know how her relationship with Keats developed during these weeks before Christmas, though there are clues in two later remarks. Keats later wrote to her that 'the very first week I knew you I wrote myself your vassal; but burnt the Letter as the very next time I saw you I thought you manifested some dislike to me.' And Fanny, writing later to Fanny Keats, recalled that the Christmas Day they spent together (for Mrs Brawne invited Keats) 'was the happiest day I had ever then spent.'

But meanwhile, there was the question of Keats' poetry. *Hyperion*, which was largely written as he watched over his dying brother, was soon to be abandoned. He wanted to do something different, and didn't want to lead a social life. He wrote to Woodhouse, who intended to introduce him to people, and put it quite bluntly: 'look here Woodhouse–I have a new leaf to turn over–I must work–I must read–I must write–I am unable to afford time for new acquaintances–I am scarcely able to do my duty to those I have.'

The house where Keats stayed in Chichester with Dilke's parents, in mid-January 1819

One of these acquaintances was Isabella Jones. Keats visited her before going on holiday with Brown to stay with some relatives of the Dilkes in Chichester. Isabella, with her sophisticated and independent ways, must have seemed a very different person from the girlish Fanny. We can make what we like of the trium-phantly sprightly lyric 'Hush, Hush! Tread softly!'; its heroine is called Isabel, and it seems to indicate a much closer relationship with Mrs Jones than had been allowed at their meeting in October. It is a poem about a sexual encounter whose secret warmth is achieved by the deception of inimical old age; and this also is the situation, if not the theme, of *The Eve of St Agnes*, which Keats wrote on the suggestion of Isabella Jones.

'The Eve of St Agnes'

On St Agnes' Day itself, 21 January 1819, after spending the night in town, Keats caught the early morning coach to Chichester, where he met Brown and their hosts, who must have been curious to see Keats. Mrs Dilke had written to her parents-in-law, 'you will find him a very odd young man, but good-tempered and very clever indeed.' For his part, Keats was obviously much impressed by Chichester, whose medieval air would have reminded him of his happy visit to Oxford eighteen months before.

In *The Eve of St Agnes* Isabella Jones' first suggestion,

> *how, upon St Agnes' Eve,*
> *Young virgins might have visions of delight,*
> *And soft adorings from their loves receive*
> *Upon the honey'd middle of the night,*

was combined with the story of Romeo and Juliet, with much of the emotion of the lyric 'Hush, hush!', and finally with a variety of other reading, such as

94

Chichester, looking across to the cathedral and its massive free-standing bell-tower

The twelfth-century crypt of Vicars' Hall, one of the remarkable medieval buildings of Chichester which form the composite background to *The Eve of St Agnes*. In Keats' time it was a wine-cellar

The Triumph of Death in the Campo Santo at Pisa, one of the engravings by Carlo Lasinio which Keats saw at Haydon's. 'I do not think I ever had a greater treat out of Shakespeare–full of Romance and the most tender feeling–magnificence of draperies . . . But Grotesque to a curious pitch . . . even finer to me than more accomplish'd works–as there was left so much room for Imagination.' The contrasts here between the lovers in a bower and the hermits, between the living and the dead–plenty and austerity, life and death–are fundamental to *The Eve of St Agnes*

French romances, Chatterton, and Coleridge. It is a sharply visual poem, and we are often reminded of Keats' tastes in the visual arts, how he frequently preferred sculptures or engravings to paintings–works of art that were the products of a hard tool rather than a brush. The strongly-cut engravings after medieval paintings in the Campo Santo at Pisa, which he had seen in Haydon's studio, provide many of the visual images, as also, in a less precise way, do Chichester itself and the atmosphere of the neighbouring chapel at Stansted, where Keats and Brown attended a service. We may associate the sculpted quality of the poem's imagery with the fact that this is one of the most worked-over and revised of Keats' poems.

Isabella Jones' suggestion was a brilliant one, and Keats was immediately responsive to it. There are many indications that he cared greatly for *The Eve of St Agnes*, and we can imagine that part of the attraction of writing the poem, aside from pleasing Mrs Jones, was that he could now rewrite and improve upon *Isabella; or The Pot of Basil*, which had disappointed him. But this was only one

96

of the ways in which he was now able to go back over his past career. He had not written in a Spenserian stanza since his very first poetry, and in determining to do so again he naturally looked back to early enthusiasms, and looked back at them to reject them. To George he wrote that 'Mrs Tighe and Beattie once delighted me – now I see through them and can find nothing in them – or weakness.' Beattie's argument for using a Spenserian stanza in his *Minstrel* was that 'it seems, from its Gothic structure and original, to bear some relation to the subject and spirit of the poem', and 'admits both simplicity and magnificence of sound and language.' In a way, this seems to apply much more to Keats than it did to Beattie, for Keats' poem is medieval, is uncomplicated in theme and expression, and at the same time is splendid in all its accessories.

Like *Isabella* and like *Lamia*, but to a greater degree, *The Eve of St Agnes* relies on straight juxtaposition between the warmth of love and the cold hostility of the rest of the world, between youth and age, between light and darkness, between passion and celibacy. Its central theme is direct, and directly stated, with a frankness that caused Taylor and Woodhouse some embarrassment, and its detailing is immensely rich, especially in the treatment of colour – with *Lamia*, it is one of the most colourful poems in English – and in such finely wrought perceptions as

> *The carved angels, ever eager-eyed,*
> *Star'd, where upon their heads the cornice rests,*
> *With hair blown back, and wings put cross-wise on their breasts.*

The chancel of Stansted Chapel, built by Lewis Way to further the conversion of the Jews. Keats and Brown went to the consecration on 25 January 1819; Keats found it 'not amusing', but he remembered some of the visual details

97

One might, indeed, note Leigh Hunt's remarks on this poem, since he hit upon the sureness of its practice and recommended its technique (so unlike his own) to all aspiring young poets:

> Let the student of poetry observe, that in all the luxury of the Eve of St Agnes there is nothing of the conventional craft of artificial writers; no heaping up of words or similes for their own sakes or for the rhyme's sake; no gaudy commonplaces; no borrowed airs of earnestness; no tricks of inversion; no substitution of reading or of ingenious thoughts for feeling or spontaneity; no irrelevancy or unfitness of any sort.

Back in London in February 1819 Keats had to deal with Abbey, who was taking Fanny away from school and even trying to curtail correspondence between her and her brother. Keats wanted more money from Abbey, not only for his own needs, but also to lend to the importunate Haydon, who was hard pressed by debts. Haydon had a rather lordly air about his friends' money, and his insensitivity about it was to lead to a break in their friendship. Keats ran into Woodhouse, who about this time was beginning to compile his very useful notes on Keats and his poetry; they shared a bottle of claret. He went to see Isabella Jones, and she suggested to him the theme of a poem that in some way belongs with *The Eve of St Agnes. The Eve of St Mark* is a delightfully fresh and limber fragment which again looks back to the medieval atmosphere of Chichester; it derives from Coleridge's *Christabel* and even more from Chatterton, whose metre and movement it reproduces. *The Eve of St Mark* has been called the first Pre-Raphaelite poem, and it was greatly appreciated by the poets of the mid-nineteenth century. Dante Gabriel Rossetti, a great admirer of Keats, was probably correct in his guess that the poem

'The Eve of St Mark'

East window of Stansted Chapel. The Jewish symbolism—seven-branched candelabra, Ark of the Covenant, etc.—found its way into *The Eve of St Mark*, where a manuscript is said to contain

The stars of Heaven, and angels' wings, . . .
Moses' breastplate, and the seven
Candlesticks John saw in Heaven, . . .
And the Convenantal Ark,
With its many mysteries,
Cherubim and golden mice.

Frontispiece to the third volume of Thomas Chatterton's works (showing the church of St Mary Redcliffe in Bristol), from the set belonging to Charles Cowden Clarke which Keats used. Such Romantic medievalism, visual as well as literary, appealed greatly to Keats

was based on the superstition that, if one watched near the lych-gate of a church on St Mark's Eve, there would appear the figures of all those who would be ill during the next year, as they passed into the church; and only those who were to recover from their illness would reappear. As the poem was left and put aside after only a hundred lines, there is no means of telling; perhaps Keats, though initially attracted to this legend, abandoned it for want of a story-line, as had happened on some occasions before.

In London Keats saw his old friend and tutor Charles Cowden Clarke, who later recalled him as being something of the belligerent schoolboy of old; he had been fighting with a butcher's boy who was tormenting a kitten. But in late February and March Keats was generally bored, irritable and nervous; even his friends got on his nerves. In mid-March he was playing cricket on the Heath. A bumper blacked his eye and he went home to bed. He wrote a sonnet, almost bitter, almost like a snarl, beginning 'Why did I laugh to-night?'. Its thin emotion jars on our knowledge of his character until we come to the end, where a kind of premonition seizes us; for here is the line,

Yet would I on this very midnight cease.

We immediately look forward to the *Ode to a Nightingale* which he was to write a month later; but we also begin to think of his own death. From this time whether thinking of Keats' poetry or of his life, we know death to be close. He writes about it, not now with a contrast between the death of the bedesman and the love of

99

Porphyro and Madeline, so full of promise as they flee from the castle; but rather with a fusion of these opposites which is to lead to that disturbing emotion, the wish to 'possess' Fanny Brawne at the very moment of his own death.

It is one measure of Keats' poetic greatness that this identification of love with death, sometimes sweet, sometimes grand, creates a poetic world that 'evaporates all disagreeables', and universalizes the factual conditions of his own life and his specific literary inspirations. An example of this was his next poem. Towards the end of April 1819 Keats wrote his famous ballad *La Belle Dame Sans Merci*. Knowing Keats' life as we do, we can tell that this poem contains the disillusion-ment (expressed with vicious rage in a letter to George) he felt in discovering that Tom's schoolfriend Charles Wells had, by way of a jest, been sending Tom fake love-letters – some of which, indeed, contained unsubtle parodies of some of Keats' earlier poetic excesses. This discovery was not precisely the occasion of the poem, but it certainly had a great deal to do with it, as some careful studies of his mood at the time have shown. The text of the poem does not indicate this; and the lesson is surely that the poetic experience, for Keats as for so many others, was a calming one. The literary influences are clearer, but the poem is so complete with its own personality that they are perhaps only striking to the literary historian. There is

'La Belle Dame Sans Merci'

Samuel Taylor Coleridge, by
Washington Allston

something of the bare plainsong of *Lyrical Ballads* in it, but with a lyricism that sings with a voice that is not Wordsworth's, and fantasy that is less excitable than than of Coleridge.

Keats had met Coleridge walking on Hampstead Heath a few days beforehand, and the philosopher-poet had treated the poet with one of his lengthy disquisitions on a variety of highly intellectual topics. But Coleridge, according to one story, said of their meeting 'there is death in that hand', and this brings us once more to the overwhelmingly poignant fact of Keats' life. Twenty-three years old now, without a wife, without children – 'the roaring of the wind is my wife and the Stars through the window pane are my Children' – Keats had a singularly palpable apprehension of death, an almost tactile feeling for it. This is something that is found in the most sensuous of natures, and appears strongly in poets – Shakespeare and Hopkins are others – with an intense feeling for the 'inscape' of the physical world. It was the sensually felt world of spring and the physical proximity of Fanny, living in the Dilkes' half of the house with her family, that lifted him from his depression. Just as the *Ode to Maia* had jumped away from a period of despondency at the end of his holiday in Devon the year before, so now does the *Ode to Psyche*.

It is almost impossible not to think of the *Ode to Psyche* as a preparation for the greater odes that were soon to follow, and it is indeed a poem about poetic dedication, celebrating the human soul as it encounters what Keats currently called the world, 'the vale of soul-making':

The odes

> *Yes, I will be thy priest, and build a fane*
> *In some untrodden region of my mind . . .*

In the next few weeks he wrote the *Ode to Indolence*, the *Ode to Melancholy*, the *Ode to a Nightingale* and the *Ode on a Grecian Urn*. They are deeply philosophical poems, more so than anything he had written before, and they can thus be regarded as belonging to this 'untrodden region of my mind'. But they are also related quite specifically to the circumstances of his life. Many of the thoughts in the long journal-letter to George that he had begun on 14 February (and did not send until 3 May) are picked up, developed, and given a poetic shape – as we immediately realize when reading such sentences in that letter as 'Neither Poetry, nor Ambition, nor Love have any alertness of countenance as they pass by me: they seem rather like three figures on a greek vase.' The odes also capitalize on the rich store of his recent poetic career, as is only natural in poems that are concerned with philosophic and aesthetic impulses and are auto-dramatic in their address, in their 'Greeting of the Spirit'. And the odes, like so much else that he wrote, are thick with references to his current reading and his life. We can feel the weather in them, for instance, and it comes as no surprise to find that they were written in a beautiful period of spring, a spring that came early in 1819 with roses already blooming by

3 May, and nightingales all over the heath—a kind of forward spring weather that has a sudden dusk unlike the long evenings of summer. This can be felt in the *Ode to a Nightingale*; and we also have Brown's account of the poem's origin. It is one of those occasions when we are quite startled by the simple and quotidian circumstances of the genesis of something we are used to thinking of as complex and eternal:

> In the spring of 1819 a nightingale had built her nest near my house. Keats felt a tranquil and continual joy in her song; and one morning he took his chair from the breakfast-table to the grass-plot under a plum-tree, where he sat for two or three hours. When he came into the house, I perceived he had some scraps of paper in his hand, and these he was quietly thrusting behind the books. On inquiry, I found those scraps, four or five in number, contained his poetic feeling on the song of the nightingale.

These four odes (together with that *On Autumn*, which was written later in the year) are commonly regarded as the summit of Keats' poetic achievement, and perhaps as the greatest short poems in Romantic literature. Yet they were written when he was only twenty-three years old, when he had been writing seriously for little more than three years. We may recall that, only a few months before, he had planned an ambitious programme for a ten-year-long development.

Whereas the *Ode to Psyche* is a poem with such a tabor-skipping and airy quality that it seems removed from the world, the *Ode to a Nightingale* opens with an almost oppressive sense of reality, not only the reality of nature, in Hampstead springtime, but also of the terrible blow which had fallen in the previous autumn, Tom's death. It is not only a world of flowers, but a world 'Where youth grows pale, and spectre-thin, and dies'. The first three stanzas of the *Ode to a Nightingale* are concerned with Keats' attempts to leave the world, and to join the nightingale on some imagined higher plane. As he does so, 'on the viewless wings of Poesy', he imagines the loss of the physical world, and sees himself dead—he uses an abrupt, almost brutal word for it—as a 'sod' over which the nightingale sings. The contrast between the immortal nightingale and mortal man, sitting in his garden, is made all the more acute by an effort of the imagination. As Keats introduces the one image he has never before employed in his poetry, that of Ruth, and follows this by the wonderful idea of

> *Charm'd magic casements, opening on the foam*
> *Of perilous seas, in faery lands forlorn*

we are aware that he has travelled into mythic realms far beyond the apprehensions of human life, and that some return must be made. And so it is, in the last stanza,

A page from Keats' manuscript of the *Ode to a Nightingale,* written in May 1819. ▶
Before publication he altered words in lines 16 and 17

Ode to the Nightingale

My Heart aches and a ~~painful~~ drowsy numbness ~~falls~~
My sense, as though of hemlock I had ~~drunk~~ pains
Or emptied some dull opiate to the drains
One minute ~~since~~ past and Lethe wards had sunk
Tis not through envy of thy happy lot
But being too happy in thine happiness
~~That~~ thou light-winged dryad of the trees
In some melodious plot
Of beechen green, and shadows numberless
Singest of summer in full-throated ease.
O for a draught of vintage that has been
Cooling an ~~age~~ long age in the deep-delved earth
Tasting of Flora, and the country green
~~and~~ Dance, and Provencal song and sunburnt mirth
O for a Beaker full of the warm south,
full of the true and blushful Hippocrene
With clustered bubbles winking at the brim
And purple stained mouth
That I might drink and ~~leave~~ the world unseen
And with thee fade away into ~~the~~ forest dim
Fade far away, dissolve and quite forget
What thou among the leaves hast never known
The weariness, the fever and the fret
Here, where Men sit and hear each other groan
Where palsy shakes a few sad last grey hairs
Where ~~is~~ ~~~~ grows pale and thin heavy and ~~~~
and dies

Some of the influences on the *Ode on a Grecian Urn*. (*Right*) A drawing by Keats of the Sosibios Vase, in the Louvre. (*Below left*) *The Sacrifice at Lystra*, engraved after Raphael's cartoon. (*Left*) *View of Delphi with a Procession,* a mezzotint after Claude Lorrain:

What little town by river or sea shore,
Or mountain-built with peaceful citadel,
Is emptied of its folk, this pious morn?

Keats also remembered the sacrifice scenes from the Elgin Marbles (see p. 38)

as the nightingale reverts to a natural, not symbolical, identity, and disappears over the next hill.

The *Ode on a Grecian Urn* deals with many of the same ideas as does the *Nightingale* ode, and it does so with a perfectly just symbol of the reality and yet intangibility of the realm of art, a symbol for which Keats had been preparing for some time, in his studies of Greek myth, in his conversations with Haydon, in his examination of folios of classical remains and of a reproduction of Raphael's cartoon *The Sacrifice at Lystra* (which Haydon discussed at some length in *The Examiner* in the first two weeks of May); and especially perhaps in all his memories of the experience of seeing the Elgin Marbles. The urn takes on all these values which can only be felt in life, as Keats so well knew, through a feeling for the artistic life, in the sense that he formulated it in his notions of 'Negative Capability'. Only thus will the urn reveal itself as being, in the phrase Keats had used before about poetry, 'a friend to man'.

In contrast to these poems, the *Ode on Melancholy* must seem a slighter production, although in some ways it is a tighter and more logically structured poem. In it there is not the same flight of the imagination; indeed this is eschewed in favour of an emphasis on embracing the mortal condition, combining (as had already been argued in *Endymion*) joy and sorrow. Melancholy is not just a 'fit', nor is it a mood, but rather a state of mind in which these opposites may be brought together.

As the three-week spell of fine weather in which he wrote the odes came to an end, Keats was brusquely reminded of his life's troubles. George wrote from America, in grave financial difficulties. There was no money to help him – or, to be more precise, the Keats family money was so enmeshed by legal difficulties and Abbey's recalcitrant handling that it seemed almost impossible to get at. There was also the question of Fanny Brawne. Wentworth Place is a small house; living on either side of it, close together and yet separated by one wall, both Keats and Fanny must have felt some kind of strain. There was no formal engagement, for Keats was hardly in a position to offer the security of a home and an income.

These considerations pushed him towards schemes for making money out of writing, and Brown, who liked money, decided to help him, and to take half. He proposed a collaboration on a verse play. Keats found this an attractive idea. His Scottish friend certainly knew something about the theatre, and had once made £300 out of a production at Drury Lane. Keats was also stimulated by the thought of Shakespeare, and by a renewed interest in the minor Elizabethan and Jacobean dramatists that had been fostered by two men he knew, Charles Lamb and Charles Wentworth Dilke. He also wanted to write for Kean's acting, which had always made such an impression on him. Brown was to supply the plot and the stagecraft, Keats the verse.

Keats' veneration for Shakespeare, whom he 'dared' to consider the 'good Genius presiding over' him, appears in the seal he used at various times between 1817 and 1819 (*above left*), and in his choice of an inkstand

For his play, *Otho the Great*, Keats felt 'There is no actor can do the principal character besides Kean.' 'Kean delivers himself up to the instant feeling, without a shadow of thought about anything else.' (*Right*) Kean in *A New Way to Pay Old Debts* by Massinger, whose works were in Keats' mind at the time

(*Below*) 'Bards of passion and of Mirth', Keats' apostrophe to the playwrights Beaumont and Fletcher written in a copy of their works, glorifies the playwright's role

221

THE FAIR MAID OF THE INN.

A TRAGI-COMEDY.

The Commendatory Verses of Gardiner ascribe this Play to Fletcher alone. It was first published in the folio of 1647; and has not been acted many years, nor, we believe, ever altered.

PROLOGUE.

PLAYS have their fates, not as in their true sense
They're understood, but as the influence
Of idle custom madly works upon
The dross of many-tongu'd opinion.
A worthy story, howsoever writ,
For language, modest mirth, conceit or wit,
Meets oftentimes with the sweet commendation
Of 'hang't! 'tis scurvy!' when for approbation
A jig shall be clapt at, and every rhime
Prais'd and applauded by a clamorous chime.

Let ignorance and laughter dwell together!
They are beneath the muses' pity: hither
Comes' nobler judgments, and to those the strain
Of our invention is not bent in vain:
The Fair Maid of the Inn to you commends
Her hopes and welcomes; and withal intends
In th' entertains to which she doth invite ye,
All things to please, and some things to delight ye.

PERSONS REPRESENTED.

MEN.
DUKE of Florence.
ALBERTUS, Admiral of Florence.
BAPTISTA, a brave Sea Commander, ancient Friend to Albertus.
CESARIO, a young Gentleman of a fiery nature, Son to Albertus.
MENTIVOLE, Son to Baptista, Lover of Clarissa.
PROSPERO, a noble Friend to Baptista.
Host, the supposed Father of Biancha.
FORORNOSCO, a cheating Mountebank.
CLOWN, the Mountebank's Man, and Setter.
DANCER,
TAILOR,
MULETIFIER,
PEDANT,
CLERK,
COXCOMB,
} Six Fools and Knaves, who pretend love to Biancha.

SECRETARY to the Duke.
TWO MAGISTRATES of Florence.
PHYSICIAN.
SURGEON.
THREE GENTLEMEN.
SAILORS.

WOMEN.
MARIANA, Wife to Albertus, a virtuous Lady.
CLARISSA, Mariano's Daughter, in love with Mentivole.
JULIANA, Niece to the Duke of Genoa, Baptista's second Wife.
BIANCHA, the Fair Maid of the Inn, beloved of Cesario, and Daughter to Baptista and Juliana.
HOSTESS, the supposed Mother of Biancha.

SCENE, Florence.

VOL. III. T t ACT

Shanklin   He told Fanny Brawne that he was going away to work, to live quietly, and to attempt to raise his fortune. He would, of course, write to her; and he would be back. He decided to go to the Isle of Wight, and caught the coach to Portsmouth on 27 June taking with him a rough scheme for the opening of the play, which was set in the bloody and turbulent times of the first Holy Roman Emperor, and was entitled *Otho the Great*. At Shanklin he lodged with James Rice, and wrote hard, despite a nagging sore throat and a feverish cold. He not only wrote the first act of the play, but also half of *Lamia*, the mysterious but vivid romance whose story had been suggested to him by Burton's *Anatomy of Melancholy*.

'Lamia'   The *Anatomy of Melancholy* was one of Keats' favourite books, and in it he read the following:

> Philostratus . . . hath a memorable instance . . . which I may not omit, of one Menippus Lycius, a young man 25 years of age, that going betwixt Cenchreas and Corinth, met such a phantasm in the habit of a fair gentlewoman, which taking him by the hand, carried him home to her house, in the suburbs of Corinth, and told him she was a Phœnician by birth, and if he would tarry with her, *he should hear her sing and play, and drink such wine as never any drank, and*

Shanklin, from the Down. To his sister on 6 July Keats wrote, 'Our window looks over house tops and Cliffs onto the Sea, so that when the Ships sail past the Cottage chimneys you may take them for weathercocks.' Ten days later, he told Fanny Brawne that he hoped to 'take a look farther about the country, and spy at the parties about here who come hunting after the picturesque like beagles.' Keats and Brown made sketches of the church

James Rice

no man should molest him; but she being fair and lovely, would live and die with him, that was fair and lovely to behold. The yong man, a philosopher, otherwise staid and discreet, able to moderate his passions, though not this of love, tarried with her a while to his great content, and at last married her, to whose wedding, amongst other guests, came Apollonius; who, by some probable conjectures, found her out to be a serpent, a lamia; and that all her furniture was like Tantalus gold . . . no substance, but meer illusions. When she saw herself descried, she wept, and desired Apollonius to be silent, but he would not be moved, and thereupon she, plate, house, and all that was in it, vanished in an instant.

Keats was excited by this story, and not only because it responded to something in his own feelings for a poetical subject; he also felt that it would be a success with the public – another indication that he was thinking in terms of gaining financial security through his writing. 'I am certain that there is that sort of fire in it which must take hold of people in some way', he wrote. Keats also had a new stylistic model for his relation of the story of the deceived Lycius. Especially in its first half, the poem is greatly indebted to Dryden, and to the great seventeenth-century poet's mastery of the heroic couplet – that couplet which Keats had dismissed years before with a jeer at its 'rocking-horse' rhythm, and which he now found so useful for the terse and rapid way in which he rewrote Burton. It is verse that pushes its way busily forward, even when it stops to luxuriate:

> *She was a gordian shape of dazzling hue*
> *Vermilion-spotted, golden, green, and blue;*
> *Striped like a zebra, freckled like a pard,*
> *Eyed like a peacock, and all crimson barr'd;*
> *And full of silver moons, that, as she breathed,*
> *Dissolv'd, or brighter shone . . .*

With a story such as that he found in Burton, it was inevitable that his poem should deal with deception and disillusionment, and throughout the poem we are conscious of a kind of bitterness, a feeling that love and poetry are somehow unreal, that their comforts cannot last, nor survive examination. There is the cynical couplet

Love in a hut, with water and a crust
Is – Love, forgive us! – cinders, ashes, dust . . .

There is also the confused condemnation of 'philosophy', presented as if it were in some way the message of the fable (some people have felt that it was). What Keats does here is to replace the exclamation of the young brother in *Comus*, 'How charming is divine philosophy, Not harsh and crabbed as dull fools think, But musical as is Apollo's lute' – which is what he really thought of philosophy ever since staying with Bailey in Oxford – by a flashy reminder of that jesting and drunken evening with Charles Lamb, when they baited Wordsworth, the most 'philosophical' (in Keats' sense) of all his contemporaries:

Do not all charms fly
At the mere touch of cold philosophy?
There was an awful rainbow once in heaven:
We know her woof, her texture; she is given
In the dull catalogue of common things.
Philosophy will clip an Angel's wings . . .

In such passages, where the quality of the verse plummets, there is evidence of an unwillingness to have anything to do with precisely those topics which he had recently come to treat with a loving seriousness. The poem must, therefore, when compared with the other productions of 1819, seem superficial: Keats was denying, even as he seemed to exalt them, both his love of love and his love of poetry.

It was not simply a question of writing for money, although we may feel that this had something to do with it. It was also a part of his troubles with Fanny. *Letters to* At precisely the time that he was at work on *Lamia*, we find him writing to her, *Fanny Brawne* urgently, passionately, and often, nastily. These letters, perhaps the most famous love-letters in the English language, record only the indecisions and pains that arose from their separation. He wanted to be with her and yet he had chosen to leave her. He was fervently absorbed in her, and yet was concentrating on his poetry, two hundred miles away (and we might note how very little of his poetry is addressed directly to her). And so he writes, 'it seems to me that a few more moments thought of you would uncrystallize and dissolve me – I must not give way to it – but turn to my writing again – if I fail I shall die hard – O my love, your lips are growing sweet again to my fancy – I must forget them.' With every abasement before her beauty, with every declaration of his love, there is also an element of rejection. Thoughts of death reappear: 'I have two luxuries to brood over in my

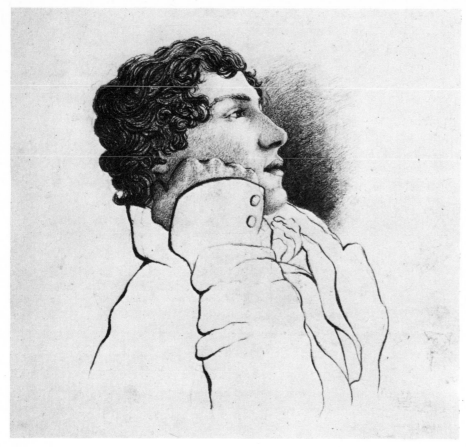

Keats drawn by Charles Brown at Shanklin, in July 1819

walks, your Loveliness and the hour of my death. O that I could have possession of them both in the same minute.' Fanny must have been puzzled and troubled by such contradictory vehemence, no less than by the hot and nasty jealousy that often appears in the letters and which—almost certainly without foundation—led some nineteenth-century commentators to consider her a harmless flirt, toying with the poet's affections. This was not the case, and if there were difficulties between them, these difficulties were largely Keats' creation.

Meanwhile, Rice went back to town, Brown joined Keats at Shanklin, and they settled down to concentrated work on *Otho the Great*. But *Lamia* was stuck. Keats wanted to read up some books to stimulate his descriptions of the wedding-feast. They decided to go to Winchester, where they stayed for some time, Keats *Winchester* working on *Lamia* and also on a play that was suggested by the atmosphere of the

III

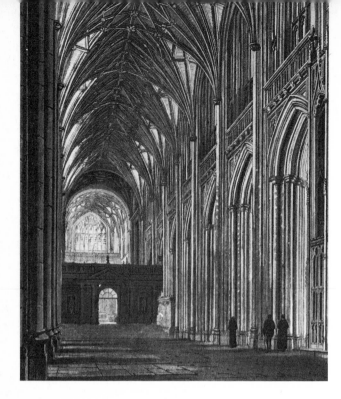

(*Left*) 'At Winchester I shall get your Letters more readily; and it being a cathedral city I shall have a pleasure always a great one to me when near a Cathedral, of reading them during the service up and down the Aisle' (Letter to Fanny Brawne, 5 August 1819)

(*Right*) The meadows between Winchester and St Cross, part of Keats' favourite daily walk. In the distance is Winchester Cathedral

city, *King Stephen*. He wrote three scenes, but on hearing that Kean, for whom the play was designed, was leaving for a tour of America, abandoned them. His own money situation, like George's who had now written again about the estate, was desperate. In an atmosphere of crisis, Keats finished *Lamia* and rushed up to London to see his publishers, Taylor and Hessey, and their adviser Woodhouse. He did not go to see Fanny Brawne, but wrote to her, posting the letter in the City. 'Am I mad or not?' he wrote, 'I love you too much to venture to Hampstead, I feel it is not paying a visit, but venturing into a fire . . . I am a Coward, I cannot bear the pain of being happy . . .' He went back to Winchester instead, and gradually he became calmer.

The summer was ending. Keats had found a favourite walk in and around Winchester which he described in some detail in his letters. It took him out from the medieval town to St Cross through meadows by the side of the River Itchen. On 19 September, a Sunday, he marvelled at the weather, and wrote afterwards to Reynolds: 'How beautiful the season is now – How fine the air. A temperate sharpness about it . . . I never lik'd stubble fields so much as now – Aye better than the chilly green of the Spring. Somehow a stubble plain looks warm – in the same way that some pictures look warm – this struck me so much in my Sunday's walk that I composed upon it.' The composition was that most peaceful of poems, the last of the great odes, *To Autumn*.

In some ways he was in a reflective mood, in others he was undecided. He wrote to Reynolds, 'To night I am all in a mist; I scarcely known what's what – But you knowing my unsteady & vagarish disposition, will guess that all this turmoil will be settled by tomorrow morning. It strikes me tonight that I have led a very odd sort of life for the two or three last years – Here & there – No anchor . . .' He put aside *The Fall of Hyperion*, which he was also writing at Winchester, and wrote letters, to George and Georgiana, to Reynolds, Woodhouse, Dilke and Brown. He asked the Dilkes to find him lodgings in Westminster – deliberately separating himself from Fanny – and he announced to Woodhouse that he intended to take up journalism. This particular resolve – in the event he did nothing about it – may well have been made because he had just abandoned another poem, just as he had abandoned *Calidore, Sleep and Poetry, Hyperion*, and *The Eve of St Mark*. This was *The Fall of Hyperion: a Dream*, the lines which have been described by a modern critic as 'Keats' final effort, an effort both cool and feverish, to discover his own poetic identity.'

This deeply mysterious fragment germinated during Keats' stay on the Isle of Wight, when he was also writing *Lamia* and *Otho the Great*, and was largely written in the calmer days in Winchester in the early autumn. Here is another approach to a fane, as in so many of Keats' philosophical poems – we can even think of the urn, or the nightingale, as being such temples – and it is approached

'The Fall of Hyperion'

113

through another of the Keatsian vales of life. Moneta, the veiled priestess at its altar, is knowledgeable of all mysteries, and can calm all strife by her knowledge. She reveals that the temple is all that remains after the war between the gods and the Titans, and she reveals herself, parting the veils:

> *Then saw I a wan face,*
> *Not pin'd by human sorrows, but bright blanch'd*
> *By an immortal sickness which kills not;*
> *It works a constant change, which happy death*
> *Can put no end to; deathwards progressing*
> *To no death was that visage; it had pass'd*
> *The lily and the snow . . .*

The description is concerned with immortality; but it feels as if Keats knew something more of death, which by its nature cannot admit of report, than any living man can see or comprehend; it is a final effort of imagination.

London and Fanny Brawne   Back in London on 8 October, he went up to Wentworth Place from his new lodgings at 25 College Street, Westminster. Fanny was there; they met; it was terrible. He was dazzled, giddied. For days he went back and forth between Hampstead and Westminster. From Westminster he wrote 'My Creed is Love and you are its tenet', but in his copy of Burton he scribbled cynical comments against love and against marriage. Within a fortnight matters were more or less

The west end of College Street, Westminster, much decayed since Keats lived there. He stayed in the house with the 'To Let' sign

Westminster in Keats' time: Parliament was still housed in a jumble of small buildings, to the left. College Street lies on the far side of the Abbey

settled. He would move back to live in Brown's half of Wentworth Place. It was settled that there was some kind of engagement to be married, even though their marriage might be far in the future. Love had won, we might feel. But what had love been fighting against? Against the demands of poetry? Or the conventions of a society that demanded financial solidity in a suitor? Or against the febrile and tortuous ambages of Keats' disturbed spirit? If Fanny's letters to Keats had survived, or if we knew more about what passed between them at happier times, like that first Christmas Day they spent together, the answers to these questions might be clearer. On the evidence we have, it might seem that the uncontrolled and unreasoning violence of Keats' love was the cause of all their troubles. Fanny's own judgement should therefore be recorded:

That his sensibility was most acute, is true, and his passions were very strong, but not violent, if by that term violence of temper is implied. His was no doubt susceptible, but his anger seemed rather to turn on himself than others, and in moments of greatest irritation, it was only by a sort of savage despondency that he sometimes grieved and wounded his friends. Violence . . . was quite foreign to his nature. For more than a twelvemonth before quitting England, I saw him every day, often witnessed his sufferings, both mental and bodily, and I do not hesitate to say that he could never have addressed an unkind expression, much less a violent one, to any human being.

12   If Nature escape not punishment, surely thy *will* shall not
        avoid it.

All this is true, say you, and who knowes it not? but how
easy a matter is it to answer these motives, and to make an
anti-parodia quite opposite unto it? To exercise myself, I will
essay.

1   Hast thou meanes? thou hast one to spend it.
2   Hast none? thy beggery is increased.
3   Art in prosperity? thy happiness is ended.
4   Art in adversity? like Job's wife shee'l aggravate thy
        misery; vexe thy soule; make thy burden intollerable.
5   Art at home? shee'l scold thee out of doores.
6   Art abroad? if thou ,be wise keep thee so; shee'l perhaps
        graft hornes in thine absence; scowle on thee coming
        home.
7   Nothing gives more content then solitariness; no solitari-
        ness like this of a single life.
8   The band of marriage is adamantine; no hope of loosing
        it; thou art undone.
9   Thy number increaseth, thou shalt be devoured by thy
        wives friends.
10   Thou art made a cornuto by an unchast wife; and shalt
        bring up other folkes children in stead of thine owne.
11   Paul commends marriage, yet he preferres a single life.
12   Is marriage honourable? What an immortall crown be-
        longs to virginity?

So Siracides himself, speaks as much as may be, for and
against women; so doth almost every philosopher plead *pro*
and *con*; every poet thus argues the case (though what cares
vulgus hominum what they say?) so can I conceive, peradven-
ture, and so canst thou. When all is said, yet since some be
good, some bad, let's put it to the venture. I conclude therefore
with Seneca.

———— cur Toro viduo jaces?
Tristem juventam solve: nunc luxus rape,
Effunde habenas, optimos vitæ dies
Effluere prohibe.

Why dost thou lye alone, let thy youth and best dayes to passe
away? Marry whilst thou maist, *donec virenti canities abest
morosa*, whilest thou art yet able, yet lusty,

ª Elige cui dicas, tu mihi sola places,

ª Ovid.

VOL. II.   2 E

Keats' notes in his copy of *The Anatomy of
Melancholy*, and the engagement ring which
he gave Fanny Brawne (photographed on
one of her muslin scarves)

The painters William Hilton (*left*) and Peter de Wint. Both men were among the personal friends who gave money for Keats' expenses in Italy

Keats was back in Hampstead, near the girl he loved. But he was disturbed and unwell. He was feeling the cold and his throat gave him trouble. He had written nothing for two months. Abbey had released some money from Tom's inheritance, with which he had paid off debts, but a regular supply of money seemed as far away as ever. He had heard nothing from the management of Drury Lane about *Otho the Great*. Fanny was just next door, but in a sense was immeasurably distant. Brown, in the next room to his own, was sleeping with their Irish housekeeper, Abigail O'Donaghue. Between playfulness and laziness, Keats wrote part of a satirical and comic poem, *The Cap and Bells*. He also took pleasure (as do many literary men) in the conversation of painters, and often went to see Peter de Wint and William Hilton at their joint home and studio in Percy Street, Rathbone Place. George came to England to deal with his finances, and together they went to see old friends, but the brothers had hardly time to catch up with each other before George got the boat back again. *The Cap and Bells* petered out.

Illness

South End Green, between Pond Street and Wentworth Place

At the beginning of February 1820, coming back from town late at night, he left the coach at Pond Street, the nearest stop to Wentworth Place, and staggered as he tried to walk. At first Brown thought he was drunk as he entered the house; but Keats was obviously ill. Brown sent him to bed, following him up the stairs:

> I entered his chamber as he leapt into bed. On entering the cold sheets, before his head was on the pillow, he slightly coughed, and I heard him say – 'that is blood from my mouth' I went towards him; he was examining a single drop of blood upon the sheet. 'Bring me the candle, Brown; and let me see this blood.' After regarding it steadfastly, he looked up in my face, with a calmness of countenance that I can never forget, and said, 'I know the colour of that blood; it is arterial blood; – I cannot be deceived in that colour; – that drop of blood is my death-warrant; – I must die.'

It was a single spot of blood, but he knew what it meant. Then he coughed more, and more blood came, quantities of it, as though he were vomiting; he thought he might suffocate; it was in his mouth, his throat; he couldn't breathe for it. The doctor came, and then he slept. In the next couple of days, as he lay limp and exhausted in bed, friends visited him. Fanny was 'a little silent'. His fever returned for a few days, but a week after the attack he went out into the garden a little. It was felt that his weakness was something that should not be too much disturbed by the emotional strain of seeing Fanny. Sometimes she sat with him, sewing, but mostly she wrote him notes, even a simple 'Good night' to hold in his hand or put under the pillow as the candles were extinguished and Brown shut his door. Sometimes a sofa was made up for him in the front parlour. As the spring approached he seemed stronger, and was able to go to town to dine with Taylor. On another occasion he went to see Haydon's picture *Christ's Entry into Jerusalem* at its first public exhibition in Piccadilly.

For two months, however, Keats was mostly in bed or around the house. Brown always let his side of Wentworth Place during the summer, and for a time he persuaded himself that it would do no harm to Keats to move him from the middle of May; he even thought that Keats might accompany him to Scotland, if they travelled there by boat. This was out of the question: Keats was not well enough. He went to live a few doors away from Leigh Hunt in Kentish Town,

No. 2 Wesleyan Place, Kentish Town,
newly built when Keats stayed here
from 4 May to 23 June 1820

Tuesday Morn –

My dearest Girl,

I wrote a letter for you yesterday expecting to have seen your mother. I shall be selfish enough to send it though I know it may give you a little pain, because I wish you to see how unhappy I am for love of you, and endeavour as much as I can to entice you to give up your whole heart to me whole whole existence hangs upon you. You could not step or move an eyelid but it would shoot to my heart – I am greedy of you – Do not think of any thing but me. Do not live as if I was not existing. Do not forget me – But have I any right to say you forget me? Perhaps you think of me all day. Have I any right to wish you to be unhappy for me? You would forgive me for wishing it, if you knew the extreme passion I have that you should love me – and for you to love me as I do you, you must think of no one but me; much less write that sentence. Yesterday and this morning I have been haunted with a sweet vision.

Letter to Fanny Brawne, written from Kentish Town in May 1820

Keats on a makeshift day-bed at the Hunts',
in Mortimer Terrace, Kentish Town. Hunt's
wife Marianne was an enthusiastic cutter of
silhouettes

after seeing Brown off to Scotland. Fanny was only a mile away, but they did not
see each other very often; he saw more of Severn, who lived in Islington. He wrote
bad letters to Fanny, one 'because I wish you to see how unhappy I am for love of
you.' He denied his friends, he accused her, he raged with impotent jealousy: 'if
you still believe in dancing rooms and other societies as I have seen you – I do not
want to live.' He regretted such outbursts, he apologized, they spoke their love to
each other, but what was there to do?

Keats could not write poetry; he had not done so for months. He corrected some
proofs for his next book, but not really with that eagerness and pride in his own
work that had previously led him to argue with Woodhouse over the cuts in *The
Eve of St Agnes*. In late June he had another bad haemorrhage, and moved from
his lodgings into Hunt's noisy house, where he lay in bed as Hunt worked on his
new journal *The Indicator*. He wrote to Fanny as if he wanted to wound her for
her life and femininity: 'Hamlet's heart was full of such Misery as mine when he
said to Ophelia "Go to a nunnery, go, go!" Indeed I should like to give up the
matter at once – I should like to die. I am sickened at the brute world which you
are smiling with.' That kind of bitterness often appears while he was at Hunt's,
but tears were more appropriate. After one of Fanny's letters had failed to reach
him he somehow got himself from Kentish Town to Hampstead. In Well Walk
he was seen uncontrollably sobbing, not walking, but just standing there. He had

121

ple as antly - O what a misery it is to have an
intellect in splints! My love again to Fanny - tell
Tootts I wish I could pitch her a basket of grapes -
and tell Sam the fellows catch here with a line a
little hoik much like an anchovy, pull them up fast

Mrs Brawne
Wentworth Place
Hampstead Middx
England

Remember me to Mrs Dilke - mention to Brown that
I wrote him a letter at Portsmouth which I did not send
and am in doubt if he ever will see it.

my dear Mrs Brawne
yours sincerely and affectionately

good bye Fanny! god bless you   John Keats -

Part of Keats' last letter to Wentworth Place, written to Fanny Brawne's mother when the
Maria Crowther was in quarantine in the Bay of Naples

just enough strength to get to Wentworth Place. Mrs Brawne took him in immediately. It was the first time he had slept in the Brawnes' house. He stayed there for a month, before he went to Italy.

To keep Keats alive, it was thought, he would have to be in the sun, in Italy. *To Italy* Shelley had asked him not long before to stay with him at Pisa, but he did not want to be with Shelley. Ill people know what they do not want to do more clearly than what they want to do, and Keats surrendered himself to the plans of his close friends, especially Taylor. He would go to Rome, would see a doctor there, would rest, maybe for a year. He would be accompanied. But who would go there with him? Brown was away in Scotland while Keats, nursed by Fanny, suffered further haemorrhages, and did not get back to London in time. In the event, Severn was asked, and the painter immediately and willingly agreed to go. There was an element of urgency about it all. They had to get the boat quickly. We do not know how Keats parted from Fanny. In her *Literary Pocket Book*, Hunt's publication which he had given to her, she simply wrote against the date, 'Mr Keats left Hampstead'. She gave him a keepsake, a cornelian, something he could hold in his hand.

On 17 September Keats, together with Severn, seen off by only three friends, boarded the *Maria Crowther* and sailed down the Thames estuary, round the coast

'The Maria Crowther, sailing brig', a watercolour by Severn showing the ship on which he and Keats voyaged to Italy. They shared the single cabin – partitioned by a screen – with two women, one a girl of 18 who was, like Keats, in an advanced state of consumption

of Kent and towards the Isle of Wight. Here he wrote a letter to Brown, thinking of death and thinking of Fanny:

> The thought of leaving Miss Brawne is above every thing horrible – the sense of darkness coming over me – I eternally see her figure eternally vanishing. Some of the phrases she was in the habit of using during my last nursing at Wentworth Place ring in my ears – Is there another Life? Shall I awake and find all this a dream? There must be we cannot be created for this sort of suffering.

It took three weeks to get to Italy, Severn devotedly nursing his friend, who suffered from fever and from further haemorrhages, and whose physical collapse was all too clearly accompanied – his friends had been forced to face this for months past – by the breakdown of his personality. In the Bay of Naples they had to wait aboard for ten more days to fulfil quarantine regulations. They went ashore on Keats' birthday; he was twenty-five. From Naples, in a specially hired carriage, it took another week to get to Rome. The English doctor there, James Clark, had already taken rooms for them in the Piazza di Spagna, just at the bottom of the Spanish Steps. Keats rested, and was able to go for short walks about Rome. But, as he wrote to Brown on 30 November, 'I have an habitual feeling of my real life having past, and that I am leading a posthumous existence.'

On 10 December Keats coughed two cupfuls of blood, was in delirium for twenty-four hours, and then had five more haemorrhages in the following nine days. He raved through his past life, he begged Severn to let him kill himself with laudanum. On Christmas Day, letters arrived from home, one of them from Fanny; he cast them aside unopened. He came to the final stages of his illness, too feeble now to rail against his condition. His body was taken with shuddering, his teeth

124

'O what an account I could give you of the Bay of Naples if I could once more feel myself a Citizen of this world–' (Letter to Mrs Brawne written in quarantine; see p. 122)

Keats reading in his bunk on board ship, after a lost sketch by Severn

Piazza di Spagna in Keats' time. The upper windows of the house on the right, No. 26, are those of the apartment he shared with Severn; his room was on the corner

Keats on his deathbed. At the bottom Severn noted '28 Janr. 3 o'clock mng. Drawn to keep me awake – a deadly sweat was on him all this night.'

chattered uncontrollably, he was covered in cold sweats. He asked Severn to place Fanny's letters in his grave. They had decided that it would be in the Protestant cemetery, and Keats asked that the stone above him should bear only the legend, 'Here lies one whose name was writ on water'. On Friday 23 February 1821, at four o'clock in the afternoon, he called 'Severn – Severn – lift me up for I am dying – I shall die easy – don't be frightened – thank God it has come.' His friend, who two summers before had been with him when Keats watched the wind ruffling the fields of ripe corn and cried 'The tide! the tide!', now took the poet in his arms and held him until he breathed his last.

126

Medallion of Keats by Girometti, intended as the centrepiece for a memorial in Rome. Brown and Reynolds considered it the best likeness

The Protestant Cemetery in Rome, drawn by Samuel Palmer. Keats was buried near the Pyramid of Cestius; visiting his grave one night by moonlight, Severn came upon just such a scene—a young shepherd asleep with his head on the grave

BIBLIOGRAPHY

CHRONOLOGY

NOTES ON THE PICTURES

INDEX

◀ The death mask

There are two great scholarly biographies of Keats, the first by Walter Jackson Bate (1964), and the second by Robert Gittings (1968). Professor Bate's book provides the fuller discussion of the poems, while Mr Gittings' volume marshalls an unparalleled wealth of local detail, as also does his earlier *John Keats: The Living Year* (1954), which is a vastly enjoyable work. An essential source book is the two-volume *The Keats Circle* (1948) edited by H. E. Rollins, who has also edited a major edition of the letters (1958). The standard text of the poems is that provided by the second edition by H. W. Garrod (1958). Other useful works are the biographies of Leigh Hunt by Edmund Blunden (1930) and of Fanny Brawne by Joanna Richardson (1952). Willard B. Pope has edited Haydon's diary (1960–63). Edmund Blunden has also written a biography of Taylor, *Keats' Publisher* (1936). An edition of Leigh Hunt's *Autobiography* was published by J. E. Morpurgo in 1949. Ian Jack's *Keats and the Mirror of Art* (rev. ed. 1968) draws attention to the influence on Keats of the visual arts, and has suggested several illustrations in this book.

1795 31 October(?): born Moorfields, London.

1803 Goes to Clarke's school, Enfield.

1810 Apprenticed to Thomas Hammond, Edmonton.

1815 Registered at Guy's Hospital.

1816 Spring: meets Severn.
May: first published poem, *To Solitude*, in Leigh Hunt's *Examiner*.
August: visits Margate.
October: writes sonnet *On first looking into Chapman's Homer*. Meets Hunt, Haydon, Reynolds.
December: Hunt writes article on 'Young Poets', bracketing Keats with Shelley. Meets Shelley. Finishes 'Sleep and Poetry'.

1817 Spring: meets Bailey, Rice, the Dilkes.
March: first book published. Finally leaves hospital. Moves to Well Walk.
April: goes to the Isle of Wight, begins *Endymion*.
May–June: visits Margate, Canterbury, Hastings. Meets Isabella Jones.
September: stays with Bailey in Oxford.
November: finishes *Endymion* at Burford Bridge.
December: meets Wordsworth.

1818 January–February: attends Hazlitt lectures at Surrey Institution.
March: goes to Teignmouth. Writes to Isabella Jones.
April: *Endymion* published.
June: accompanies George and Georgiana Keats to Liverpool. Goes on walking tour with Brown.
August: returns to London to find Tom ill.
September: begins *Hyperion*.
November: had met Fanny Brawne.
December: Tom dies. Moves to Wentworth Place.

1819 January: goes to Chichester. Writes *Eve of St Agnes*.
May: writes great odes.
June–July: stays at Shanklin. Begins *Lamia, Otho the Great*.
August: moves to Winchester. Writing *The Fall of Hyperion*.
October: returns to live in Wentworth Place.

1820 February: first haemorrhage.
May–August: stays in Kentish Town.
July: second volume of poems published.
September: leaves for Italy.
November: reaches Rome.

1821 23 February: dies in Rome.

Frontispiece: JOHN KEATS, aged 21; detail of a page from the diary of Benjamin Robert Haydon, 19 November 1816. Haydon drew Keats on the agreement that Keats would draw him (for the result, see p. 29). From a facsimile at Keats House, Hampstead.

5 GEORGE KEATS (1797–1841); miniature by Joseph Severn, 1817. Keats-Shelley Memorial House, Rome.

TOM KEATS (1799–1818); sketch by Joseph Severn, 1817. Keats-Shelley Memorial House, Rome.

FANNY KEATS Y LLANOS (1803–1889); portrait by her son Juan, 1860s. Keats House, Hampstead. *Photo Eileen Tweedy.*

6 SWAN AND HOOP livery stables and public house (in the projection bottom left); plan from the City of London's 'lease to Mr John Jennings' (Keats' grandfather) 'of two Messuages or Tenements on the West side of Moorfields and several stables coach houses and buildings in the Swan and Hoop Stable Yard', 8 November 1786. The Swan and Hoop lay between Little Moorfields (now Moorfields)–where its frontage was 117 feet

long–and Moorfields (now Finsbury Pavement), just north of Fore Street (now London Wall). It had vanished by 1875. By courtesy of the Corporation of London Records Office.

LIVERY STABLES of T. Chew & Son (reached through the covered passage at the left) and King's Arms public house, on the west side of Little Moorfields, London; watercolour, 1849. British Museum, London. *Photo Eileen Tweedy.*

7 THE BUILDING which housed John Clarke's school at Enfield; photograph taken between its conversion into a railway station in the 1840s and its demolition in 1872. The central section of the upper storey is preserved in the Victoria and Albert Museum, London. Keats House, Hampstead.

8 INSPECTION of the Honourable Artillery Company in September 1803; detail of aquatinted etching. British Museum, London. *Photo Eileen Tweedy.*

9 KEATS' COPY of *The English and the French Languages Compared,* by Duverger (1807), one of his books at Clarke's school. Keats House, Hampstead. *Photo Eileen Tweedy.*

133

10 THOMAS HAMMOND'S SURGERY, next to his house in Edmonton (demolished); photograph, *c.* 1890. Keats House, Hampstead.

THOMAS HAMMOND'S HOUSE, in Church Street, Edmonton (demolished); photograph, 1890. At the far right, behind the trees, is one of the two surgery buildings (right, in the previous illustration). Keats House, Hampstead.

11 COUNTRY near Enfield; lithograph, 1844. British Museum, London. *Photo Eileen Tweedy.*

12 CHARLES COWDEN CLARKE (1787–1875); portrait by an unknown artist, *c.* 1834. National Portrait Gallery, London.

13 TWO PAGES from Keats' copy of Spenser's *Faerie Queene* (reduced), showing typical annotations – underlining, lines in the margin, and a cross. Houghton Library, Harvard University.

15 NORTH FRONT of Guy's Hospital, London; engraving, 1815. Keats House, Hampstead. *Photo Eileen Tweedy.*

BOROUGH HIGH STREET to Dean Street, Southwark; detail from *Horwood's Plan of London Westminster and Southwark*, 1813. Visible lower left are some of the vast coaching inns which were common in Southwark. Almost all the area shown has been rebuilt since Keats' time. Guildhall Library, London. Reproduced by courtesy of the Corporation of London. *Photo R. B. Fleming.*

16 HENRY STEPHENS; portrait in the former Louis A. Holman Collection. From the collection of Holman negatives in Keats House, Hampstead.

GEORGE FELTON MATHEW; silhouette. From a facsimile at Keats House, Hampstead.

17 EDMONTON; engraving for Dr Hughson's *Description of London*, 1806. Keats House, Hampstead. *Photo Eileen Tweedy.*

HIGH STREET, SOUTHWARK (Borough High Street), looking west from a spot near the end of St Thomas' Street (see map, p. 15); detail of a lithograph by George Scharf, 1830. The east side of the street was then in process of demolition. British Museum, London. *Photo Eileen Tweedy.*

18 'TO SOLITUDE'; detail of page from *The Examiner*, May 1816 (enlarged). Keats House, Hampstead. *Photo Eileen Tweedy.*

19 JOHN KEATS; sketch by Joseph Severn, 1816. Victoria and Albert Museum, London (Crown copyright).

DETAIL OF PAGE from the notebook Keats kept as a medical student (slightly enlarged). Keats House, Hampstead. *Photo Eileen Tweedy.*

20 CERTIFICATE of the Society of Apothecaries awarded to Keats on 26 July 1816. From a facsimile at Keats House, Hampstead.

21 BATHING AT MARGATE; engraving by J. Shury after G. Varlo, 1820. Public Library, Margate, Kent. *Photo L. W. Bamberger.*

22 BOAR'S HEAD PLACE, formerly the Boar's Head Inn, on the east side of Southwark High Street just north of St Thomas' Hospital; watercolour by T. H. Shepherd, 1832. The street was then due for demolition. British Museum, London. *Photo Eileen Tweedy.*

23 MANUSCRIPT of *On first looking into Chapman's Homer*, written in October 1816 (slightly reduced). Houghton Library, Harvard University.

24 LEIGH HUNT (1784–1859); sketch by Thomas Wageman, February 1815. National Portrait Gallery, London.

25 HAMPSTEAD and West End; detail from *Cruchley's New Plan of London and its Environs*, 1830 edition (identical with the edition of 1828 for this area). Guildhall Library, London. Reproduced by courtesy of the Corporation of London. *Photo R.B. Fleming.*

26 VALE OF HEALTH, Hampstead Heath; watercolour by F.J. Sarjent, 1804. Keats House, Hampstead. *Photo Eileen Tweedy.*

27 BACCHUS AND ARIADNE, by Titian. Keats certainly knew an engraving, and may well have seen the painting itself when it was exhibited at the British Institution. Reproduced by courtesy of the Trustees of the National Gallery, London.

THE TRIUMPH OF FLORA; etching after Poussin, by Chataigner. *Photo Courtauld Institute of Art, University of London.*

28 CHRIST'S ENTRY INTO JERUSALEM, by Benjamin Robert Haydon, 1819. St Gregory Seminary, Cincinnati, Ohio.

29 BENJAMIN ROBERT HAYDON (1786–1846); self-portrait sketch, 1816. Victoria and Albert Museum, London (Crown copyright).

PAGE from the diary of Benjamin Robert Haydon with sketches which include a drawing of Haydon by Keats (in profile, centre top); probably dating from 19 November 1816, when Haydon drew

Keats (see Frontispiece). From a facsimile at Keats House, London.

30 JOHN HAMILTON REYNOLDS (1794–1852); miniature by Joseph Severn. From the collection of the late Walter Sichel, reproduced by courtesy of Miss Penelope Sichel. *Photo National Portrait Gallery, London.*

JOHN HAMILTON REYNOLDS; silhouette in the former Louis A. Holman Collection. From the collection of Holman negatives at Keats House, Hampstead.

31 CHEAPSIDE, London, looking west; engraving after T.H. Shepherd, 1831. British Museum, London. *Photo Eileen Tweedy.*

33 LIFE-MASK of Keats made by Haydon shortly before 17 December 1816 (electrotype). National Portrait Gallery, London.

34 FEMALE OPERATING THEATRE of Old St Thomas' Hospital, London; constructed in 1821 in the roof of the hospital chapel (now the Chapter House of Southwark Cathedral), later abandoned, and recently restored. It is the only surviving early 19th-century operating theatre. *Photo copyright Photographic Department, Guy's Hospital, London.*

35 PERCY BYSSHE SHELLEY (1792–1822) writing *Prometheus Unbound* in the Baths of Caracalla, Rome; painting by Amelia Curran. Keats-Shelley Memorial House, Rome.

36 JOSEPH SEVERN (1793–1879) at the age of 29; detail of self-portrait pencil sketch. Keats House, Hampstead. *Photo Eileen Tweedy.*

WILLIAM HAZLITT (1778–1830); detail of chalk drawing by William

Bewick, 1825. National Portrait Gallery, London.

37 TITLE PAGE of *Poems* by John Keats, published by C. and J. Ollier in 1817; from the copy belonging to Charles Brown, with his signature. Keats House, Hampstead. *Photo Eileen Tweedy.*

38 DETAIL of the south frieze of the Parthenon, showing a heifer led to sacrifice. Reproduced by courtesy of the Trustees of the British Museum, London.

39 TEMPORARY ELGIN ROOM at the British Museum; painting by A. Archer, 1819. Reproduced by courtesy of the Trustees of the British Museum, London.

40 JOHN TAYLOR (1781–1864); detail of portrait by William Hilton, *c.* 1817. Collection R. C. Taylor. *Photo courtesy Heinemann Educational Books Ltd.*

JAMES AUGUSTUS HESSEY (1785–1870); detail of portrait by William Hilton, *c.* 1817. Collection Mrs Sylva Blunden. *Photo courtesy Heinemann Educational Books Ltd.*

41 PAGE from Keats' seven-volume set of Shakespeare (printed by C. Whittingham, Chiswick, 1814; actual size), showing annotations at the end of *A Winter's Tale*. Houghton Library, Harvard University.

43 DIANA AND ENDYMION; paste gem made by James Tassie, recorded in his catalogue for 1791 (enlarged). Victoria and Albert Museum, London (Crown copyright).

44 CARISBROOKE CASTLE, Isle of Wight; engraving by W. B. Cooke after W. Alexander, 1814. British Museum, London. *Photo Eileen Tweedy.*

ENTRANCE to the cathedral close at Canterbury (with the pre-Victorian façade of the cathedral visible in the distance); engraving by J. Le Keux, *c.* 1828. British Museum, London. *Photo Eileen Tweedy.*

45 NEW ENGLAND BANK INN at Bo Peep, between Hastings and St Leonards, Sussex; from a photograph of a print of *c.* 1833/6 (location of original unknown). Hastings Public Library.

46 WELL WALK, Hampstead; drawing by Hastings, *c.* 1820. Keats House, Hampstead. *Photo Christopher Oxford, courtesy Heinemann Educational Books Ltd.*

47 HAMPSTEAD HEATH; detail of watercolour by John Varley, 1826. Keats House, Hampstead. *Photo Eileen Tweedy.*

48 OXFORD from the meadows; engraving after W. Westall, *c.* 1830. British Museum, London. *Photo Eileen Tweedy.*

49 BENJAMIN BAILEY (1791–1853); watercolour. Keats House, Hampstead. *Photo Eileen Tweedy.*

OLD MAGDALEN HALL and Grammar School, Oxford; etching by J. Fisher, 1820. Reproduced by permission of the President and Fellows of Magdalen College, Oxford. *Photo courtesy Heinemann Educational Books Ltd.*

50 SHAKESPEARE'S BIRTHPLACE, Stratford on Avon; engraving, 1806. British Museum, London. *Photo Eileen Tweedy.*

51 FRONTISPIECE to Jeremy Taylor, *The Rule and Exercises of Holy Living*, 1651. British Museum, London. *Photo Eileen Tweedy.*

52 BOX HILL and Burford Bridge, Surrey; detail of engraving from *The Beauties of England and Wales*, c. 1806–10. 'I like this place very much–There is Hill & Dale and a little River' (letter to Reynolds, 22 November 1817). British Museum, London.

53 GLAUCUS AND SCYLLA; etching after Salvator Rosa by H. Winstanley, 1728. British Museum, London. *Photo Eileen Tweedy.*

54 HORACE SMITH (1779–1849); engraving after a portrait by Masquerier, from A. H. Beavan, *James and Horace Smith*, 1899. Keats House, Hampstead. *Photo Eileen Tweedy.*

55 WILLIAM WORDSWORTH (1770–1850); chalk drawing by Benjamin Robert Haydon, 1818. National Portrait Gallery, London.

56 CHARLES WENTWORTH DILKE (1789–1864); detail of portrait, artist and date unknown. On loan to Keats House, London, reproduced by kind permission of Lady Dilke. *Photo Eileen Tweedy.*

57 WENTWORTH PLACE (now Keats House), Hampstead, from the front and back. The house was made into a single dwelling and enlarged by an extra wing in 1839. Above, *photo Mainwaring Photographs Ltd.* Below, from the collection of Holman negatives in Keats House, Hampstead.

58 JOHN KEATS; miniature by Joseph Severn, February–March 1819. National Portrait Gallery, London.

59 JOHN KEATS; sketches in Benjamin Robert Haydon's diary, made on 19 November 1816. When later asked by Elizabeth Barrett Browning for a drawing of Keats, Haydon provided stylized 'Greek' versions like the smaller sketch. From a facsimile at Keats House, Hampstead.

60 'CONTENDING FOR A SEAT'; etching by Theodore Lane, 1820s. Victoria and Albert Museum, London (Crown copyright).

61 EDMUND KEAN as Richard II (Act IV, Scene 4); detail of painting by John James Halls, 1814. Victoria and Albert Museum, London (Crown copyright).

62 DRURY LANE THEATRE, London; engraving by W. Hopwood after N. Heiddoff, 1813. Victoria and Albert Museum, London (Crown copyright).

63 TWO PAGES from Keats' copy of *The Characters of Shakespear's Plays*, by William Hazlitt (published by C. and J. Ollier, London, 1817; reduced), showing Keats' annotations on the discussion on *King Lear*. Houghton Library, Harvard University.

64 CHARLES LAMB (1775–1834); watercolour portrait by George Francis Joseph, 1819. British Museum, London. *Photo Eileen Tweedy.*

CHARLES JEREMIAH WELLS (1800–1879); heliogravure by Emery Walker after a miniature. Keats House, Hampstead.

66 DEATH ON THE PALE HORSE; painting by Benjamin West, completed 10 October 1817. The Pennsylvania Academy of the Fine Arts, Philadelphia.

67 SURREY INSTITUTION, London (demolished); aquatint by Rowlandson and Pugin, 1809, from Ackermann's *Microcosm of London*. British Museum, London. *Photo Eileen Tweedy.*

Notes

RICHARD WOODHOUSE (1788–1834) as a child; artist and date unknown. Houghton Library, Harvard University.

68–9 THE ENCHANTED CASTLE (*Landscape with Psyche at the Palace of Cupid*), by Claude Lorrain. Reproduced by permission of the Trustees of T.C. Loyd. *Photo Courtauld Institute of Art, University of London.*

VIEW of the entrance of the river Teign, Devon, looking across to Teignmouth; aquatint, 1818. Keats House, Hampstead. *Photo Eileen Tweedy.*

71 GEORGIANA (1801/2–1879) AND GEORGE KEATS; silhouettes, *c.* 1830. Reproduced by courtesy of Miss Ella Keats Whiting. *Photo Chalue.*

72 MAP of the route followed by Keats and Charles Armitage Brown through the north of England, northern Ireland and Scotland. From the collection of Holman negatives in Keats House, Hampstead.

74–5 SADDLEBACK and part of Skiddaw; watercolour by John Constable, 21 September 1806. In Book IV of *Endymion* Keats writes:

Or from old Skiddaw's top, when fog conceals
His rugged forehead in a mantle pale,
With an eye-guess towards some pleasant vale
Descry a favourite hamlet faint and far.

Victoria and Albert Museum, London (Crown copyright).

BOWNESS and Windermere; engraving by W. Le Petit after T. Allom, British Museum, London. *Photo Eileen Tweedy.*

CHARLES ARMITAGE BROWN (1787–1842); detail of bust by Andrew Wilson, 1828. Keats House, Hampstead. Reproduced from a negative in Keats House.

THE MARKET PLACE, Ambleside; painting by Julius Caesar Ibbetson, 1817. Art Gallery and Temple Newsam House, Leeds.

76 GREYFRIARS' CHURCHYARD, Dumfries; engraving after W.H. Bartlett, 1830s. British Museum, London. *Photo Eileen Tweedy.*

77 DETAIL OF LETTER from John Keats to his brother Tom, written from Scotland on 17 July 1818 (reduced). Keats House, Hampstead. *Photo Eileen Tweedy.*

78 MARIA DILKE (d. 1850); miniature. Reproduced by kind permission of Sir John Dilke.

DETAIL OF PAGE from Keats' large copy of Shakespeare (facsimile reprint of the First Folio of 1623, published in 1803; enlarged). Keats presented the book to Fanny Brawne in 1820, before his departure for Italy. Keats House, Hampstead. *Photo Eileen Tweedy.*

79 FIRST PAGE of the six-page review of *Endymion* in *Blackwood's Edinburgh Magazine* for August 1818, published on 1 September (actual size). Keats House, Hampstead. *Photo Eileen Tweedy.*

81 OPENING PAGE of Dante's *Inferno* in Henry Francis Cary's translation, from the miniature three-volume set taken by Keats on his northern tour. Beinecke Rare Book Library, Yale University.

83 ANNOTATED PAGE from Keats' copy of Milton's *Paradise Lost*, 1807 (enlarged). Keats House, Hampstead. *Photo Eileen Tweedy.*

85 FINGAL'S CAVE, Staffa; aquatint by W. Daniell, 1813. Victoria and Albert Museum, London. *Photo R.B. Fleming.*

138

86 OPENING of the review of *Endymion* in *The Quarterly Review* for April 1818, published on 27 September (actual size). Keats House, Hampstead. *Photo Eileen Tweedy.*

87 KEATS' COMMENTS on the note (by Taylor or Woodhouse) inserted at the beginning of *Lamia, Isabella, The Eve of St Agnes, and Other Poems*, published at the beginning of July 1820; from a copy presented by Keats to a neighbour in Hampstead, Burridge Davenport (actual size; text only reproduced). Houghton Library, Harvard University.

88 QUEEN SQUARE, Bloomsbury; aquatint published by R. Ackermann, 1812. Guildhall Library, London. Reproduced by courtesy of the Corporation of London. *Photo R.B. Fleming.*

89 SEAL-IMPRESSION of Mrs Isabella Jones, from one of her letters. Reproduced by permission of Messrs Brooke-Taylor and Co., Bakewell. *Photo courtesy Heinemann Educational Books Ltd.*

FANNY BRAWNE (1800–1865); silhouette by Augustin Edouart, 1829. Keats House, Hampstead. *Photo Eileen Tweedy.*

90 'GATE OF JUDGEMENT' leading to St Stephen's, Coleman Street, London (destroyed in World War II). The Jennings family vault was in the north aisle. *Photo Will F. Taylor.*

91 JOHN KEATS in his sitting room at Wentworth Place; painting by Joseph Severn, 1821. The furnishings were described to Severn by Charles Brown. National Portrait Gallery, London.

92 FANNY BRAWNE; original miniature, 1833. On loan to Keats House, Hampstead, reproduced by kind permission of

Mrs N.F. Goodsell and Mrs Oswald Ellis. *Photo Eileen Tweedy.*

93 TWO PAGES of a letter from Fanny Brawne to Fanny Keats, July 1822. Keats House, Hampstead. *Photo Eileen Tweedy.*

94 NO. 11 EASTGATE SQUARE, Chichester, the house rented by Charles Wentworth Dilke's parents (the square was then Hornet Square). *Photo Emily Lane.*

95 CHICHESTER, looking south to the cathedral; engraved by J. Greig after Storer, 1811. British Museum, London. *Photo Eileen Tweedy.*

CRYPT of Vicars' Hall, Chichester; from an old photograph, taken before the crypt's transformation into tea-rooms. National Monuments Record, London.

96 THE TRIUMPH OF DEATH; engraving by Carlo Lasinio from his *Pitture a fresco del Campo Santo di Pisa*, 1812. These were almost certainly the engravings Keats saw at Haydon's on 27 December 1818. British Museum, London. *Photo John R. Freeman.*

97 CHANCEL of Stansted Chapel, Sussex. *Photo Emily Lane.*

98 EAST WINDOW of Stansted Chapel, Sussex. *Photo courtesy Heinemann Educational Books Ltd.*

99 FRONTISPIECE to Thomas Chatterton's *Works*, Vol. III, 1803. Keats House, Hampstead. *Photo Eileen Tweedy.*

100 SAMUEL TAYLOR COLERIDGE; detail of portrait by Washington Allston, 1814. National Portrait Gallery, London.

103 PAGE from Keats' manuscript of the *Ode to a Nightingale*, written in May 1819.

Notes

Reproduced by permission of the Syndics of the Fitzwilliam Museum, Cambridge.

104 VIEW OF DELPHI WITH A PROCESSION; mezzotint by Richard Earlom after a drawing in the *Liber Veritatis* of Claude Lorrain, 1777. Collection Emily Lane.

THE SACRIFICE AT LYSTRA; engraving after Raphael by Nicolas Dorigny, early 18th C. (reversed from the original cartoon). British Museum, London. *Photo Eileen Tweedy.*

105 DRAWING or tracing by Keats of the Sosibios Vase. Keats-Shelley Memorial House, Rome.

106 SEAL-IMPRESSION made with a Tassie gem head of Shakespeare, from Keats' letter to Benjamin Bailey of 3 November 1817. Houghton Library, Harvard University.

KEATS' BRONZE INKSTAND, with a bust of Shakespeare. At his death it was sent to his brother George in America. Keats House, Hampstead. *Photo Eileen Tweedy.*

107 EDMUND KEAN as Sir Giles Overreach in *A New Way to Pay Old Debts*, by Philip Massinger; oil sketch attributed to G. Clint. Keats read Massinger avidly in 1819 and 1820. Victoria and Albert Museum, London (Crown copyright).

KEATS' COPY of *The Dramatic Works of Ben Jonson and Beaumont and Fletcher*, 1811, showing the manuscript of 'Bards of Passion and of Mirth', written before 2 January 1819. In a later rebinding the book was trimmed and part of the text lost. Keats House, Hampstead. *Photo Eileen Tweedy.*

108 VIEW from Shanklin Down, Isle of Wight; engraving by George Brannon, 1837. Keats House, Hampstead. *Photo Eileen Tweedy.*

109 JAMES RICE (1792–1832); watercolour miniature. Keats House, Hampstead. *Photo Eileen Tweedy.*

111 JOHN KEATS; pencil drawing by Charles Brown, July 1819. National Portrait Gallery, London.

112 WINCHESTER CATHEDRAL nave, looking east; detail of aquatint by D. Havell after E. Mackenzie, for Ackermann's *History of Winchester College*, 1816. British Museum, London. *Photo Eileen Tweedy.*

113 VIEW of Winchester from the meadows on the way to St Cross; engraving by Edward Finden after W. Westall, *c.* 1830. British Museum, London. *Photo Eileen Tweedy.*

114 WEST END of Great College Street (formerly College Street), Westminster; drawn by A. S. Illingworth at the time of its demolition. National Monuments Record, London.

115 'WESTMINSTER ABBEY, St Margaret's Church & the New Square from Parliament Street'; engraving, 1822. British Museum, London. *Photo Eileen Tweedy.*

116 ANNOTATED PAGE from Keats' copy of *The Anatomy of Melancholy* by Robert Burton, Vol. II, 1813 (reduced). Keats House, Hampstead. *Photo Eileen Tweedy.*

ENGAGEMENT RING given by Keats to Fanny Brawne, worn by her until her death in 1865; gold, set with an almandine (photographed on a pink embroidered muslin scarf which also belonged to Fanny

Brawne). The ring may have been Keats' mother's, but it fittingly bears the en-twined snakes symbolic of medicine. Keats House, Hampstead. *Photo Eileen Tweedy.*

117 WILLIAM HILTON (1786–1839); self-portrait. Lincoln City Libraries, Museum and Art Gallery. *Photo Lincoln Corporation.*

PETER DE WINT (1784–1849); minia-ture portrait by William Hilton. Lincoln City Libraries, Museum and Art Gallery. *Photo Lincoln Corporation.*

118 SOUTH END GREEN, at the bottom of Pond Street, Hampstead, near Wentworth Place; engraving, 1820s. British Museum, London. *Photo Eileen Tweedy.*

119 NO. 2 WESLEYAN PLACE, Kentish Town; photograph by Louis A. Holman, 1929. The street is now due for demolition. Keats House, Hampstead.

120 FIRST PAGE of a letter from Keats to Fanny Brawne, May 1820. Keats House, Hampstead. *Photo Eileen Tweedy.*

121 JOHN KEATS reading at the Hunts' in Kentish Town, June/July 1820; silhouette by Marianne Hunt. First published in *The Strand Magazine*, XII, 1896.

122 LAST PAGE–folded on the outside, with the address–of a letter from Keats to Mrs Brawne, dated 24 October 1820 (reduced). The letter is discoloured by fumigation. Keats House, Hampstead. *Photo Eileen Tweedy.*

123 THE *Maria Crowther*; watercolour by Joseph Severn, probably executed when the boat was off the English coast in September 1820. Keats House, Hamp-stead. *Photo Eileen Tweedy.*

124 PART OF NAPLES, from the bay; detail of drawing by Maria Lady Callcott, November 1818, from her album. British Museum, London. *Photo Eileen Tweedy.*

125 JOHN KEATS reading in his bunk on the *Maria Crowther*; drawn from memory by Arthur Severn after a lost sketch by his father. From Caroline Spurgeon, *Keats's Shakespeare*, reproduced by permission of the Oxford University Press.

THE SPANISH STEPS and No. 26 Piazza di Spagna; drawing by Maria Lady Callcott, February 1819, from her album. British Museum, London. *Photo Eileen Tweedy.*

126 JOHN KEATS on his deathbed; ink drawing by Joseph Severn, 28 January 1821. Severn later made several replicas of the drawing. Keats-Shelley Memorial House, Rome.

127 PROFILE PLAQUE of John Keats; by Giuseppe Girometti, 1821. Made at the request of Richard Woodhouse, based on the life-mask. Keats House, Hampstead. *Photo Eileen Tweedy.*

THE PROTESTANT CEMETERY, Rome, by Samuel Palmer. Keats House, Hampstead. *Photo Eileen Tweedy.*

128 DEATH-MASK of John Keats; original cast from the mould made on 24 February 1821. National Portrait Gallery, London.

INDEX

Page numbers in italics indicate illustrations

Abbey, Richard 8, 12, 25, 30–34 *passim*, 38, 80, 93, 98, 106, 117
Ambleside 73, 75
America, United States of 71, 88, 106, 112

Bailey, Benjamin 36, 40, 48, *49*, 50, 51, 60, 69, 71, 110
'Bards of Passion and of Mirth' *107*
Beattie, James (*The Minstrel*) 14, 97
Bentley, Benjamin 39, 90
Blackwood's Edinburgh Magazine 51, 79, 80, 87
Bloomsbury (London) *88*
Boccaccio 70
Boileau, Nicolas 32
Bo Peep (Sussex) *45*; see also Hastings
Bowness 73, *74–5*
Brawne, Fanny 56, *89*–90, *92*, 93–4, *113*–26 *passim*; engagement 115, *116*; letters of JK to 110–11, 112, 114, *120*
Brawne, Mrs Frances 93, 94, *122*, 123
British Critic, The 87
Brown, Charles Armitage 37, 55, 73, 75, 76–8, 89, 90, 94–6, 102, 106, *111*, 113, 117–26 *passim*
Burford Bridge (Surrey) 51, *52*, 62
Burns, Robert 76, 77
Burton, Robert 108, 109, 114, *116*
Byron, Lord 14, 32, 38

Calidore 18, 113
Calvinism 76
Cambridge 14
Canterbury 44, *45*

Cap and Bells, The 117
Cary, Henry Francis 76
Carisbrooke Castle (Isle of Wight) *44*, 45
Champion, The 60
Chapman, George 22, 23, 82
Chatterton, Thomas 14, 96, 98; *Works 99*
Cheapside (London) 30, *31*, 39
Chichester *94*, *95*, 96, 98
Clarke, Charles Cowden 7, 9, 10, *12*, 13–16, 20, *21*–2, 24, 37, 56, 99
Clarke, John 7, 8
Claude Lorrain 26, *68*, *104*
Coleridge, Samuel Taylor 14, 96, 98, *100*, 101
College Street *114*, 115
Cox, Jane 80
Croker, John Wilson 85

Dante 48, 76, *81*
de Wint, Peter 117
Dilke, Charles Wentworth 55, *56*, 106, 113
Dilke family *78*, 80, 94, 101
Drury Lane Theatre (London) 60, *62*, 65, 90, 106, 117
Dryden, John 14, 109
Dumfries 76

Edmonton (Middlesex) 7, 10, 16, *17*; Hammond's house and surgery *10*
Elgin Marbles *38*, *39*, 105
Eliot, T.S. 82
Endymion 18, 36, 40–43, *44*–54, 69, 70, 73, 81–2, 84, 106

Enfield (Middlesex) 10; Clarke's school 7–9, 12, 42
Epistle to Charles Cowden Clarke 20, 21–2
Epistle to George Felton Mathew 20
Epistle to my Brother George 20, 21
Eve of St Agnes, The 70, 94–8, 121
Eve of St Mark, The 98, 113
Examiner, The 10, 12, *18*, 20, 21, 25, 53, 60, 105

Fall of Hyperion, The 113–14
Fingal's Cave (Staffa) *85*
Florio, John 70

Guy's Hospital 14, *15*, 16, 34

Hammond, Thomas 9, *10*, 14
Hampstead 18, 24, *25*, *26*, 47, 89, 90, 101, 102, 112, 117, *118*; Well Walk 39, *46*, 78; Wentworth Place 56, *57*, 73, 78, 90, *91*, 106, 114–19 *passim*, 123
Hastings (Sussex) 45, 46, 53, 88
Haydon, Benjamin Robert 26–7, *28*, *29*, 30, 34, 36–8, 54, *55*, 56, 58, *59*, 65, 82, 96, 98, 105, 119
Hazlitt, William 14, *28*, 32, *36*, 37, 50, 60–*63*, 65, 66, 70, 80
Hesiod 82
Hessey, James Augustus 39, *40*, 80, 84
Hilton, William *40*, 117
Homer 65, 82
Hopkins, Gerard Manley 101
'How many bards gild the lapses of time' 16
Hunt, John 12
Hunt, Leigh 10–*24*, 25, 27, 28, 32–40 *passim*, 46–7, 51, 58, 69, 73, 87, 93, 98, 119, 121, 123
Hunt, Marianne (Mrs Leigh), silhouette of JK *121*
'Hush, hush!' 94
Hyperion 81, 82, 84, 94, 113

Indicator, The 121
Ireland 72, 77
Isabella; or, The Pot of Basil 70–71, 96, 97
Islington 88, 121

'I stood tip-toe' 37, 42
Italy 123, *124*, *125*, 126, *127*

Jones, Isabella 46, 53, 88–*89*, 94, 96, 98

Kean, Edmund 60, *61*, 62, 90, 106, *107*, 112
Keats, Edward 5
Keats, Fanny 5, 30, 43, 48, 80, 93, 94, 98
Keats, Frances Jennings 5
Keats, Georgiana Wylie (Mrs George) 71, 73, 93, 113
Keats, George 16, 89; childhood 5–8; at Cheapside 30–31; at Teignmouth 55, 69; marries and emigrates 71, 73; financial troubles 106, 112, 117; letters of JK to 21–2, 40, 56, 80, 88, 89, 92, 93, 97, 100, 101, 113; on JK 58
Keats, Thomas 5
Keats, Tom 5, 7, 65, 77, 100, 117; at Margate 20, 45; at Cheapside 30–31; at Teignmouth 55, 69–70; at Well Walk 39, 78–81; ill health 30, 39, 46, 69–70, 71, 78–81; death 90, 93, 102
Kentish Town *89*, 119–21
King Stephen 112
Knight, Richard Payne 38

La Belle Dame Sans Merci 100
Lake District 72, 73, 74–5, 76
Lamb, Charles *64*, 65, 106, 110
Lamb, Mary 65
Lamia 70, 97, 108, 109, 110, 111, 112, 113
Lemprière, John (*Classical Dictionary*) 42
Lines on the Mermaid Tavern 69
Lytton, Bulwer 85–7

Margate (Kent) 18, *21*, 32, 37, 45
Marlowe, Christopher 14
Mathew, George Felton *16*, 20, 46
Milton, John 14, 48, 65, 66, 70, 82, *83*, 110
Monkhouse, Thomas 54, 65
Moorfields (London) 5, *6*

Naples 122, *124*
Napoleon ('Buonaparte') 82, 88
'Negative Capability' 62, 63, 105

Index

Newport (Isle of Wight) 45
Newton, Isaac *28*, 65
Novello, Vincent 93

Ode to Autumn 102, 112
Ode on a Grecian Urn 34, 38, 45, 101, *104–5*
Ode to Indolence 101
Ode to Maia 71, 101
Ode to Melancholy 101, 106
Ode to a Nightingale 99, 101, 102, *103*, 105
Ode to Psyche 101, 102
O'Donaghue, Abigail 117
Ollier, Charles and James, publishers 32, *37*, 39
On first looking into Chapman's Homer 22, *23*
On Peace 14
On the Sea 45
On seeing the Elgin Marbles 38
Otho the Great 107, 108, 111, 113, 117
Oxford *48*, *49*, 50, 60, 94, 110

Pisa *96*, 123
Pope, Alexander 32
Poussin, Nicolas 26, *27*

Quarterly Review, The 85, 86, 87

Raphael 28, *104*, 105
Reynolds, John Hamilton 26, 30, 32, 35, 39, 47, 60, 68, 69, 70, 80, 88, 112, 113
Rice, James 108, *109*, 111
Robin Hood 69
Rome 37, 123, 124, *125*, 126, *127*
Rosa, Salvator *53*
Rossetti, Dante Gabriel 98
Ruskin, John 82

St Stephen's, Coleman Street *90*
St Thomas' Hospital 16, *22*, 34
Scotland 72, *76*, 77, 80, *85*, 119, 121
Severn, Joseph 5, *19*, *36*, 37, 47, *58*, 65, 121, *123–127*
Shakespeare, William 34, 40, *41*, 45, 47, 50, 62–9 passim, *78*, 82, *91*, 101, *106*
Shanklin (Isle of Wight) *108*, 111
Shelley, Mary 35
Shelley, Percy Bysshe 32, *35*, 36, 37, 69, 123

Siddons, Sarah 90
Skiddaw 74–5, 76
Sleep and Poetry 26, 27, 32, 37, 42, 113
Smith, Horace 36, *54*, 55, 69
Southampton 40, 45
Southwark *15*, 16, 17, *22*, 24, 30
Spenser, Edmund *13*, 14, 82
Stansted (Sussex) 96, *97*, *98*
Stephens, Henry *16*, 19
Stratford on Avon *50*
Surrey Institution (London) 65, 67
Swan and Hoop 5, *6*

Tassie gems *43*, *106*
Taylor, Jeremy 50, *51*
Taylor, John 39, *40*, 52, 70, 73, 88, 97, *119*, 123
Taylor and Hessey, publishers 39, 66, 112
Teignmouth (Devon) 55, *68–9*
Tighe, Mary 14, 97
Titian 26, *27*
To my Brothers 30
Tooke, J. H. (*Pantheon*) 42
'To Solitude' 16, *18*

'Unfelt, unheard, unseen' 47

Vasari, Giorgio 28
Virgil 65, 82

Wageman, Thomas *24*
Wells, Charles Jeremiah *64*, 65, 100
West, Benjamin 37, *39*, 66
Westminster 113, *114*, 115
'Why did I laugh to-night?' 99
Wight, Isle of *44*, 45, *108*, 113
Winchester 11, *112*, 113
Windermere, Lake 73, *74–5*
Woodhouse, Richard 66, 67, 69, 84, 94, 97, 98, 112, 113, 121
Wooler, Thomas (*Black Dwarf*) 12
Wordsworth, William 14, 16, *28*, 30, 48, 50, *54*, 55, 65, 73, 82, 101, 110
Written in Disgust of Vulgar Superstition 36
Written on the Day that Mr. Leigh Hunt Left Prison 14
Wylie, Georgiana *see* Keats

Few poets have equaled the dazzling achievement of John Keats. During his brief career he produced poetry that was to win him recognition as one of the outstanding poets of the English Romantic movement. Born in London in 1795, the son of a livery-stable manager, Keats had neither the advantages of birth nor the education of the other great Romantic poets. But in 1816 he met Leigh Hunt, who published some of his early verse and introduced him to a wide circle of literary and artistic friends. During the next four years he produced his greatest works, among them *The Eve of St. Agnes*, *Ode to a Nightingale*, *Ode to Autumn*, and *Ode on a Grecian Urn*, in which his wonderful music and sensuousness are evoked with complete technical mastery. While his first love was poetry, Keats was also a prolific letter writer. His letters, which are among the liveliest in our language, not only throw light on his personality but also, in their discussions of self-discovery and poetic theory, illuminate his verse.

In this new life of Keats, Timothy Hilton combines biography with literary criticism and relates both to the places that Keats knew, and to the people and books that molded his personality. Engravings, photographs, portraits, and reproductions of the poet's own manuscripts illustrate almost every stage of his career—from his childhood to the years of his growing fame as a poet, his love for Fanny Brawne, his trips in Britain, and the last tragic journey to Rome. The book offers the most complete pictorial record of Keats's life ever published, incorporating new discoveries such as a plan of the livery stables where he was born, and brings us as close as we shall probably ever come to Keats the man "in his habit, as he lived."